D0368507

PLATO'S STATESMAN

The Library of Liberal Arts
OSKAR PIEST, FOUNDER

STATESMAN

PLATO

Translated by

J. B. SKEMP

Edited, with an introduction, by

MARTIN OSTWALD

The Library of Liberal Arts

published by

Bobbs-Merrill Educational Publishing
Indianapolis

The Bobbs-Merrill Company, Inc.
4300 West 62nd Street
Indianapolis, Indiana 46268

Eighth Printing 1977
Library of Congress Catalog Card Number: 57-14633
ISBN 0-672-60230-x (pbk)

A Division of
THE BOBBS-MERRILL COMPANY, INC.
Printed in the United States of America
Library of Congress Catalog Card Number: 57-14633
ISBN 0-672-60230-X (pbk)
Seventh Printing

CONTENTS

PLATO'S STATESMAN

NOTE ON THE TEXT

The present edition of Professor J. B. Skemp's translation of Plato's *Statesman* is published with the permission of Routledge and Kegan Paul, Ltd., and the Yale University Press. The editor wishes to take this opportunity to acknowledge gratefully Professor Skemp's generosity in permitting changes to be made in the text of his translation. Some of Professor Skemp's notes have been retained either entire or in an abridged form; others were retained in altered form; and others again were contributed by the present editor. These last are identified by [Ed.] at the end of the note. All of these changes were intended to make the present edition more suitable for American classroom use. Needless to say, the responsibility for them rests with the editor.

M. O.

EDITOR'S INTRODUCTION

THE DATE OF THE *STATESMAN*

The problem of dating the dialogues of Plato has vexed many generations of scholars, because the evidence depends primarily upon the dialogues themselves rather than upon external sources. Yet thanks to the meticulous investigations of Plato's style initiated by Lewis Campbell in his famous edition of the *Sophist* and the *Statesman* (1867), it has been possible to recognize three stylistic groups in the dialogues which follow one another chronologically. There is no longer any doubt that the *Statesman* belongs to the third and last of these groups, which also includes the *Theaetetus, Sophist, Philebus, Timaeus, Critias,* and the *Laws.*

Within this third group, the date of two dialogues can be fixed with some precision. It has been convincingly demonstrated that the *Theaetetus* was written shortly after 369 B.C.,[1] and we know from ancient sources that the *Laws* was Plato's last work and that he left it unfinished when he died in 347 B.C.[2] Moreover, there are passages in the *Statesman* which imply that the *Sophist* had already been published.[3] There are also hints that the *Theaetetus, Sophist,* and *Statesman,* together with a projected but unexecuted dialogue on the *Philosopher,* were to form a thematic unit.[4] If this sequence ena-

1 Eva Sachs, *De Theaeteto Atheniensi* (Berlin 1914).

2 Olympiodorus, *Prolegomena to Plato's Philosophy* 24-25 in K. F. Hermann, *Platonis Dialogi* VI (Leipzig 1892), 218; cf. also Diogenes Laertius III, 37.

3 257a, 284b, and 286b. Unless another work is specified, all references are to the *Statesman.*

4 257a. Apart from the reference to Theaetetus at the opening of the *Statesman,* an appointment made at the end of the *Theaetetus* (210d) is kept at the beginning of the *Sophist* (216a).

bles us to place the *Statesman* within the last twenty years of Plato's life, there are philosophical and biographical considerations which make it possible to narrow its date still further.

It is well known that the three journeys to Sicily which Plato undertook exerted a crucial influence upon his thought. From the first of these, taken in 390/89 B.C., he returned to Athens filled with disgust at the luxurious life he had encountered at the court of Dionysius I, tyrant of Syracuse. What he had seen there corroborated the conviction to which the events of the late fifth century and the trial and death of Socrates had already driven him: only "on the basis of the right kind of philosophy is it possible to discern what is just in all matters, in political affairs as well as in the lives of individuals." [5] His first experience at Syracuse was to him the final proof of the utter corruption and consequent instability of the existing forms of government; [6] accordingly, upon his return to Athens he took action: he founded the Academy, where for the next forty years he searched for and taught what he considered to be the right kind of philosophy.

Plato's second visit to Sicily, in 366/65 B.C., was no doubt occasioned by the publication of the *Republic*. In this work, Plato had propounded the view that a perfect state, based upon a rational exploitation of the highest qualities in man, might be approximated in practice by entrusting the government to a philosopher-king, and that, given the right native talent and temperament, such a philosopher-king might be produced by education. These convictions evidently had made an impression on Dion, the brother-in-law and one of the chief ministers of the tyrant Dionysius, with whom Plato had struck a close friendship on his first visit to Sicily. At any rate, when Dionysius I died in 367 B.C., Dion invited Plato to come again to Syracuse and test his theory in practice by educating the young and promising Dionysius II, son and heir to his predecessor, to be a philosopher-king. The great misgiv-

[5] *Seventh Epistle* 326a.
[6] *Ibid.*, 326c-d.

ings with which Plato finally accepted the invitation are clearly stated in the *Seventh Epistle*[7] and the event showed that they were fully justified. Intrigues caused Dion to be expelled and Dion's exile, in turn, made Plato anxious to leave, though Dionysius tried his best to retain him.

When Dionysius extended a second invitation, coupled with the promise to recall Dion within a year, it was only the insistence of Dion himself and of Archytas, a Pythagorean and friend of Plato's from Tarentum, that moved Plato to undertake his third and final visit to Sicily in 361/60 B.C. Far from keeping his promise, Dionysius soon proceeded to confiscate and sell Dion's property and to place Plato under house arrest, from which he was liberated only upon the intercession of Archytas. On his return to Greece, Plato met Dion at the Olympic Games in 360 B.C. Dion vainly tried to enlist Plato's support for a forcible overthrow of Dionysius, and Plato's efforts at effecting a reconciliation between the exile and the tyrant were also of no avail. Dion managed to re-enter Syracuse by force in 357 B.C. Though he succeeded in expelling Dionysius, he was himself assassinated in 353 B.C. under somewhat obscure circumstances and by people who seem to have had some sort of connection with Plato's Academy.

This is the background into which the development of Plato's political thought from the time when he wrote the *Republic* to the writing of the *Statesman* has to be set. The belief in the perfectibility of man through education, which underlies the most characteristic parts of the *Republic*, must have received a severe jolt during his second visit to Sicily in 366/65 B.C., and it is hardly conceivable that the *Statesman* should have been written before then. This visit brought Plato into closer and more intimate contact with the actual business of governing than he ever had before; it is not surprising that his experiences should be reflected in his next major work on political theory, the *Statesman*.

What had these experiences taught him? A full answer to

[7] *Ibid.*, 328b-329a.

that question depends on a more thoroughgoing analysis of the whole work than can be given in these introductory pages. But even a cursory reading of the *Statesman* will show what Professor T. A. Sinclair has pointed out: [8] his experiences in Sicily had not mellowed Plato into being more tolerant in his ideas, but into being more tolerant toward people. The ideas propounded in the *Republic* are not given up, but Plato's attention is no longer focused upon the "pattern laid up in heaven"; rather, he deals with the degenerate states that we find here on earth and the best kind of government that can be realized among them. In other words, the belief in the perfectibility of man gradually gives way to an awareness that the frailty and fallibility of the human animal make a new approach to the problem of government mandatory: Plato has come to recognize the gulf that separates what is desirable from what actually is. We shall return to this point later on. For the moment it suffices to state that on this score alone the *Statesman* can be placed before the *Laws*, where quite a different approach to the problems of government is taken, and where Plato is concerned with framing laws to govern the degenerate societies to which he only grudgingly permits the use of laws in the *Statesman*.

If, then, we can take it as established that the *Statesman* was written after the second journey to Sicily in 366/65 B.C. and before the *Laws*, we can perhaps come closer to the exact date. Plato argues in the *Statesman* that in the best state, where a true statesman rules, the consent of the governed is of little moment: when it is in the interest of the welfare of the community, the statesman may put to death or banish any citizen who obstructs his work.[9] Professor J. B. Skemp has convincingly argued that such a view cannot well have been advocated after Plato's refusal, upon his return from his third journey, to support Dion's attempt to enter Syracuse by force,

[8] T. A. Sinclair, *A History of Greek Political Thought* (London 1952), p. 180.

[9] 293a-e, 296b-297b.

and that, accordingly, the *Statesman* must have been written before the invitation for the third journey was extended in 362 B.C.[10] Thus we can date the *Statesman* with some confidence between 365 and 362 B.C.

THE LOGICAL METHOD OF THE DISCUSSION

The Greek name of the *Statesman* is *Politikos,* which, literally taken, designates the man who has the affairs of his fellow citizens (*politai*) at heart. If we take this title at its face value and compare it with the titles of Plato's other works on political theory—the *Politeia* (*Republic,* or, more precisely, *Constitution*) and the *Nomoi* (*Laws*)—we get a small but perhaps not insignificant indication of his increased interest in people, of which Sinclair speaks.

Nevertheless, it would seem at first glance that Sinclair's statement is contradicted by the logical and methodological preoccupation with the problem of definition to which the larger part of the dialogue is devoted. After all, what does this fairly theoretical discussion have to do with governing and the man who is to govern? Many scholars have, accordingly, taken the position that the primary aim of the *Statesman* is to train the reader in the art of definition. In a sense, this is quite true, and Plato himself seems to support such a view when he makes the Stranger from Elea elicit from Young Socrates the admission that the purpose of searching for the true statesman is to make the interlocutors better dialecticians.[1] At the same time, however, it is obvious that everything said in the dialogue is indispensable for the definition of the statesman which is attained at the end. It must be remembered that for Plato the "art of statesmanship" (πολιτικὴ τέχνη) is the "royal art" (βασιλικὴ τέχνη) not only in the sense that it is the art proper to the king, but also in that it is supreme among

[10] J. B. Skemp, *Plato's Statesman* (New Haven 1952), pp. 16-17.
[1] 285d; cf. also 287a.

all the arts. Once this is realized, the fundamental importance of defining the relationship of the art of statesmanship to its subordinate and contributory arts becomes clear. To find and define the place and the nature of the truly royal art is the end for which these often tedious mental exercises are undertaken.

The method which Plato employs here to reach the definition of the statesman is explicitly stated for the first time in the *Phaedrus* (265d ff.) and is most clearly demonstrated in the *Sophist* and in the *Statesman*. Modern scholars frequently refer to it as Plato's "later dialectic" to distinguish it from the "earlier dialectic" found, above all, in the *Republic* (531c ff.).[2] There is nothing wrong with retaining this kind of description, provided we bear in mind that the difference between "earlier" and "later" is not a quantitative difference of time—for, as a matter of fact, both kinds are found together in the *Phaedrus*—but a qualitative distinction: the aim of the "earlier dialectic" is the attainment of the "Ideas" or "Essential Forms," culminating in the Essential Form of the Good, while the "later dialectic" sets itself the more modest goal of classifying and defining concepts.[3] Moreover, the exact procedure of attaining the Essential Forms or Ideas is not clearly demonstrated in the Platonic dialogues, and Plato himself states in the *Phaedrus* and in his *Seventh Epistle* that it cannot be described in writing.[4] The concept-logic, on the other hand, can be expounded in written form, and is exemplified at considerable length both in the *Sophist* and in the *Statesman*.

What procedure does this concept-logic follow and how is it exploited for the definition of the statesman? The key terms in this method are Collection (*συναγωγή*) and Division (*διαίρεσις*). In the words of the *Phaedrus*, Collection consists in "bringing together and comprehending into a unity the widely

2 The fullest modern treatment of the "earlier dialectic" is R. Robinson, *Plato's Earlier Dialectic* (Ithaca, N.Y., 1941).

3 See E. Kapp, *Greek Foundations of Traditional Logic* (New York 1942), pp. 31-36.

4 *Phaedrus* 274b-276d; *Seventh Epistle* 341b-342a.

scattered particulars."[5] Though we find only comparatively few explicit examples of Collection in the works of Plato, it is quite clear that it should always precede Division: in order to arrive at the specific form or concept, which is the object of the inquiry, we must start from some general or generic notion of the area within which the object of our search is to be found. This area is, needless to say, larger than the specific goal and includes many elements that are only loosely related to it. Once the elements have been gathered together by the process of Collection, the Division can proceed. Its object is "to divide into specific forms according to natural articulations without attempting to shatter any part, as an inefficient butcher might do,"[6] and "to know how to distinguish, kind by kind, in what ways the several particulars can combine and in what ways they cannot."[7] In other words, the differences which are brought to light at each stage in the Division must be *real* and not accidental, they must differentiate one specific form from another in a significant and meaningful way.[8] When the process has been completed and constant division[9] and subdivision have brought us to the specific form which we set out to seek, the applicable parts which have been retained in the various stages of Division can be brought together so as to form the completed definition. The purpose of this method which, as even a cursory reading of the *Statesman* will show, is as complex as it sounds simple, is to avoid faulty generalizations by subjecting each new stage to a close scrutiny on the basis of the results already attained: each new stage must draw *significant* distinctions if its result is to be valid. That is the reason why the first process of Division in the *Statesman*[10] is interrupted approximately at its half-way mark by an excursus

5 *Phaedrus* 265d.

6 *Ibid.*, 265e.

7 *Sophist* 253d-e.

8 See especially the discussion at 262a-263b.

9 For the sake of clarity, the present translation uses the capital initial for the process of Division (διαίρεσις) as such, and the small initial for each stage in that process when a division or "cutting" is made.

10 258b-268d.

on the importance of dividing correctly: it is as wrong to divide mankind into Greeks and barbarians as it would be to make a division of number by separating 10,000 from all other numbers.[11] We shall see in the next section how exactly the method of Division is made to serve the definition of the kingly ruler in the *Statesman.*

THE PLACE OF THE *STATESMAN* IN PLATO'S POLITICAL THEORY

The demonstration of the correct use of Division is not Plato's primary purpose in the *Statesman.* The first process of Division, as we shall see, leads straight into a self-criticism of Plato's previous views which he had expressed in the *Republic* some twelve or fifteen years earlier. However, the fundamental tenet, on which the whole structure of the *Republic* rests, is maintained: ruling is a "science" or "expert knowledge" (ἐπιστήμη) that is governed by certain knowable principles.[1] As in the *Republic,* Plato still cherishes in the *Statesman* the hope that a true statesman possessing such expert knowledge might arise to transform the state into a true commonwealth,[2] a hope which is all but shattered fifteen years later in the *Laws.*[3]

The criticism of the *Republic* comes out in the *Statesman* only as a result of the first attempt at defining the kind of expert knowledge which the true statesman or king has and practices. It is a theoretical science, in which the king personally directs living things that are gregarious and tame land animals which walk, and which are hornless non-interbreeding bipeds. The science of the statesman-king—the two terms are used practically interchangeably in the dialogue—thus turns out to be of the same order as the science of the herdsman.

[11] 262b-e.

[1] 258b.

[2] 301d.

[3] *Laws* IV, 711e-712a; IX, 875c.

The position of the ruler as shepherd is precisely that which the Guardians occupy in the early part of the *Republic.* The state which they govern is constructed by Socrates less as a concrete working proposal for a society that can be realized here on earth than as an "example" or "demonstration model," as it were,[4] to lay down the pattern of justice in the state, where it can be seen in larger and more readily intelligible letters than in the individual.[5] It is largely Socrates' argument with Thrasymachus which necessitates the construction of this demonstration model, and one of the essential parts of that argument involves Thrasymachus' contention that rulers govern in their own interest, just as shepherds fatten their sheep for their own profit.[6] It is interesting to note that Socrates, while rejecting this view, nowhere objects to the analogy between rulers and shepherds. In fact, he uses the self-same image later, when he likens the relation between the Guardians and the Auxiliaries to that of shepherd and dog.[7]

The first objection raised in the *Statesman* to the analogy of the king with the shepherd betrays the mark left upon Plato by contact with the practice of government, of which we have spoken before. Unlike the herdsman, whose rule over his herd is unchallenged, the position of the statesman and his right to govern is actually disputed by a host of merchants, farmers, doctors and the like, all of whom also claim to be feeders or rearers of mankind: not until the statesman has been isolated from these rivals can we assert that we have properly defined him.[8]

But this criticism is only a prelude to the onslaught against the analogy which follows in the myth.[9] The precise meaning of many details of the myth is still obscure; but there can be

[4] παραδείγματος ἕνεκα: *Republic* V, 472c.
[5] *Ibid.,* II, 368d-369a.
[6] *Ibid.,* I, 343a-347e.
[7] *Ibid.,* IV, 440d.
[8] 267e-268c.
[9] 268d-274d.

little doubt about its main point in the context here. There was a time, we are told, when the rotation of the universe was helped along by a god, and that rotation was in the opposite direction to its present movement. That era was the age of Kronos, the same age which Hesiod identifies with the "Golden Age." [10] In it not only was the rotation of the universe itself in the hands of the deity, but the government of the earth, too. The earth was at that time divided into provinces, each of which was governed by a god, and a divine daemon was set over each different kind of living being. Most important of all, men were ruled by a god in the same way as human shepherds now rule over animals and provide for all their needs. "When this god was shepherd there were no political constitutions and no personal possession of wives and children. For all men rose up anew into life out of the earth, having no memory of the past. Instead they had fruits without stint from trees and bushes; these needed no cultivation but sprang up spontaneously out of the ground without man's toil. For the most part they disported themselves in the open, needing neither clothing nor couch, for the seasons were blended evenly so as to work them no hurt, and the grass which sprang up out of the earth in abundance made a soft bed for them." [11]

However, this era now lies in the distant past; we are now living in the age of Zeus. The transition from the earlier to our present age took place when the divine pilot of the universe let go of the rudder and retired to his observation tower. At the same time, the divine rulers of the provinces here on earth also relinquished their posts. The universe, now without a guiding hand, had so much innate energy stored up within it that it began to reverse the direction of its rotation. At first, it adhered to the instructions which it had received from the god, but as time went on it abandoned them more and more. This is the stage at which we are now; and although man still has the use of the fire given him by Prometheus and the secrets

[10] Hesiod, *Works and Days,* lines 109-120.
[11] 271e-272a.

of the crafts taught him by Hephaestus and Athena, he has to shift for himself. As he gradually forsakes the divine instructions, things will go from bad to worse, until evil overshadows good to such an extent that eventually the divine pilot will take the rudder again, and gods will again look after mankind.

The application of the myth to the herdsman-king analogy is made explicit in the sequel:[12] in the age of Kronos the relation of the divine rulers to their human subjects was indeed like the relation of a shepherd to his flock. Just as the shepherd can exercise his rule over a willing herd, because he is different from and naturally superior to it, so the rule of the gods, by virtue of their natural superiority, was then accepted without question by the men who were then in their charge. It was by reason of a similar kind of natural superiority that the Guardians were said to govern in the *Republic:* like the gods in the myth of the *Statesman* they were described as shepherds; their qualities of intellect and physical stamina, symbolized by the gold in their souls, elevated them naturally far above their subjects who had only silver or an alloy of iron and brass in their souls; they further resembled the people who lived in the age of Kronos in that they claimed to be born from the earth and because they had no wives and children to call their own.[13] In other words, in relegating the shepherd-king to a distant past, when the government of the earth was divine and when the universe rotated in a direction contrary to its present course, the state of the Guardians in the *Republic* is now rejected because it does not answer to the requirements of the world as it exists under the dispensation of Zeus. We are now living in an age in which the king and statesman is a man governing men, and in which, consequently, the problem of ruling is different, since the statesman is like and not naturally superior to his subjects.

The myth of the age of Kronos is told again in very similar

[12] 274e-277a.

[13] *Republic* III, 414d-415d; V, 457b-461e.

terms in Plato's last work, the *Laws*.[14] Kronos, realizing that man is by nature inadequate to rule over men, set superior divine daemons over them, just as we do not let oxen rule oxen or goats goats, but entrust them to a man, who is naturally superior to them. Under this regime, human life was peaceful, happy, and righteous. But when a mortal rules the state, "there is no escape from evil and trouble for mankind." Accordingly, what we must do is to follow—Plato says "imitate" (μιμεῖσθαι) —by every means the life that is led under the rule of Kronos by letting ourselves be guided by the spark of immortality that is within us: we must frame *laws*, so called because they are the *leg*acy of intel*lig*ence.[15]

The interesting point to note is that any government of men by men is, in this passage of the *Laws*, rejected as bad, because it invariably leads to excesses. Instead, intelligence, which ties us to the gods and is embodied in the law, is to be supreme in the ordering of human affairs. Although, as we shall see later, the possibility of government by law is already envisaged in the *Statesman*, Plato is not yet as pessimistic about the imperfection of man as he will be in the *Laws*: he still cherishes the hope that a human being can arise who will master the science of statecraft, and whose rule will be better than the rule of law.

Who will such a man be? The herdsman-king analogy and its criticism has shown that we must not look for a godlike king, but for a ruler who can be realized in the present cycle of the universe, a man who possesses the science of ruling his own kind, the science of statesmanship.

The problem which Plato faces here is similar to one with which he had dealt in the *Republic*, and, as we shall see, there are also certain similarities in the answer. Immediately after

[14] *Laws* IV, 713b-714a. For a fuller treatment of this myth in the *Laws* and a comparison with the *Statesman*, see M. Vanhoutte, *La philosophie politique de Platon dans les "Lois"* (Louvain 1954), pp. 327-349.

[15] *Ibid.*, 713e-714a. The translation here is geared to recapture the etymologizing pun in τὴν τοῦ νοῦ διανομὴν ἐπονομάζοντας νόμον. A more literal rendering would be: "law named after the dispensation of the mind."

the outline of the state of the Guardians in the *Republic* was completed, the question of its attainability was brought up. In reply, Socrates pointed out that this state was constructed as an "example" or "demonstration model" to show the nature of absolute justice in the individual and in the state. As such, it can never be completely attained, and it is a sufficiently great achievement to approximate it as closely as possible. The least possible change which will cause existing states to begin to approximate the Guardian state is brought forward in the great paradox of the philosopher-king: "Unless either philosophers become kings in their countries or those who are now called kings and rulers come to be sufficiently inspired with a genuine desire for wisdom; unless, that is to say, political power and philosophy meet together, while the many natures who now go their several ways in one or the other direction are forcibly debarred from doing so, there can be no rest from troubles, my dear Glaucon, for states, nor yet, as I believe, for all mankind. . . ." [16]

In other words, the rule of the philosopher-king is different from that of the Guardians: while the Guardians are a group of rulers, he is to rule as an individual; and whereas the state of the Guardians remains a "pattern laid up in heaven," [17] the philosopher-king is to bring about the transformation of actually existing states here on earth to some approximation of the state of the Guardians. The fact that the larger part of the remainder of the *Republic* is devoted to a discussion of the education of the philosopher evinces Plato's conviction that the knowledge requisite for a philosophical rule is teachable and that, given the right natural endowment, a philosopher-king may conceivably be produced.

That the vision of a philosopher-king was still very much alive in the mind of Plato when he wrote the *Statesman* is shown in the way in which he describes the kingly ruler. Throughout the dialogue the conviction is expressed that there exists a science of ruling which can be attained, even if

[16] *Republic* V, 473c-d, tr. by F. M. Cornford (Oxford 1945).
[17] *Ibid.*, IX, 592b.

only by one or two outstanding individuals.[18] Moreover, the striking image of the ship's captain which describes the position of the philosopher in the *Republic* is repeated in the *Statesman* to describe the true ruler.[19] Yet in spite of this, there is one important difference: the ruler to whom the *Statesman* looks forward is no longer a philosopher. This is most explicitly indicated at the opening of the work. We are told that Plato planned to devote a separate dialogue to a discussion of the philosopher to follow the discussion of the statesman: [20] we are, therefore, justified in assuming that the science of the statesman is not identical with philosophy. Moreover, nothing is said in the dialogue about the education of the statesman, and there is not even the faintest hint that political science may be related to the Essential Form of the Good. With a significant shift in emphasis, it is now the art of weaving that is enlisted in the attempt to define the science which the statesman-king practices.

The importance which Plato himself attached to the analogy of weaving is shown by the fact that he prefaces its introduction with a discussion of the nature of "example." [21] The point of this digression is simply to warn of the pitfalls to which a false analogy exposes an argument and to state the uses of this method: it is to enable us to proceed from the familiar to an unknown which is to be defined. The analogy between shepherd and statesman has been found faulty, and the art of weaving is introduced as a new starting point for the definition of the royal ruler.

Inasmuch as the purpose of weaving is the production of clothes to protect the body, it is classified as one of the preventive arts. Just as there are many arts that contribute to the protection of man, weaving itself has a number of contributory arts—or ξυναίτια, as Plato calls them—which are distinct from weaving, yet without which weaving cannot proceed.

18 See especially 292e-293a.

19 Compare 296e-298e with *Republic* VI, 488a-489a.

20 257a-b.

21 277a-279a.

Such arts are carding, spinning, the making of warp and woof, fulling, darning and the like—in short, all the arts which provide the material foundation for the art of weaving. Now, though each of these contributory arts will consider its own work the most important, the only art that ultimately matters for the production of clothes—the true αἰτία or cause—is the art of weaving, which combines the work done separately by the contributory arts.

This analogy is now applied to the life of the state. Just as weaving is the only true causative art in the production of clothes, so statesmanship is the only true art of managing the life of the state. There are other arts without which the state cannot exist: the state needs producers of raw materials, of tools, vessels, etc.; it also needs servants, laborers, merchants, and shipowners to render various services; and there are further minor officials, such as clerks, heralds, soothsayers, and priests. Although all these arts are necessary for the exercise of statesmanship, they are only contributory to it, and the art of the statesman is superior to them all. Only the man who possesses this royal science can rule the state properly: that "queer crowd" of priests and sophists and other impersonators who now govern the various states are ignorant of this science and can never rule in any true sense of the word. Any man who masters this science, whether he actually is a ruler or not, can be called βασιλικός or "royal"—only he is the true statesman who has now been defined.

When and if such a man can attain power—when, in other words, government is in the hands of men who really know the science of statesmanship—the consent of the governed will be of no importance. "It makes no difference whether their subjects be willing or unwilling; they may rule with or without a written code of laws, they may be poor or wealthy. It is the same with doctors. We do not assess the medical qualification of a doctor by the degree of willingness or unwillingness on our part to submit to his knife or cautery or other painful treatment. Doctors are still doctors whether they work according to written rules or without them and whether they be poor or wealthy. So long as they control our health on a scientific basis, they may purge and reduce us or they may build us up, but they still remain doctors. The one essential condition is that they act for the good of our bodies to make them better instead of worse, and treat men's ailments in every case as healers to preserve life. We must insist, I think, that this alone constitutes the criterion of the science of medicine—and of any other true art of ruling as well." [22] Similarly, the statesman who masters the art of statesmanship may banish his subjects or put them to death, as long as such action is conducive to the health and welfare of the body politic. It is the task of the ruler to improve the citizens and to make them just, and every necessary means is justified in attaining this end.

The way in which the statesman proceeds in weaving the web of the state is set forth in more specific terms toward the end of the dialogue.[23] In discharging his function, the statesman is helped by the orator, the general, and the judge, whose arts, though distinct from one another and from the art of the statesman, are yet akin to statesmanship. The work of the statesman is supreme in that he has to decide when persuasion is to be used, when war is to be waged, and what the standards of justice are: the enactment and realization of his decisions are left to the practitioners of the subordinate arts. Moreover, since the supreme goal of statecraft is the achievement of unity, peace, and harmony in the state, the highest task of the statesman becomes the weaving of the aggressive and courageous warp of society to the quiet and self-controlled weft. This will be brought about by a strict regulation of marriage: a like temperament must not be permitted to marry its own kind, for this would breed the kind of excess that will destroy the fabric of the state. Only where there is a statesman who functions in this manner can the state be a true and balanced community, which shares the same ideals.

Plato ardently hoped that the rule of the true statesman would be attained. But, at the same time, there are indications

[22] 293a-c.

[23] 303d-311c.

that he realized he was hoping against hope. At the end of his discussion of the six degenerate forms of government which prevail in actually existing states, he praises monarchy as the best—"unless of course the seventh is possible [i.e., the rule of the true statesman], for that must always be exalted, like a god among mortals, above all other constitutions."[24] Just as, in the *Republic,* the state of the Guardians had to remain a "pattern laid up in heaven," the possibility of the appearance of a true statesman here is as remote as the appearance of a god among men. As we saw, the *Republic* advocated the rule of a philosopher-king to approximate the perfection of the Guardians; in the *Statesman* the kingly ruler who is the true statesman and who is modeled upon the philosopher-king becomes the desirable but probably unattainable ideal, and a government of law is proposed as an inferior second-best—inferior, because it is a mere imitation of the rule of the statesman.[25]

To describe the relation between the true statesman and the institution of written laws, Plato has recourse to the poignant analogy of the doctor who has to travel abroad.[26] Before his departure, the doctor leaves written instructions concerning the treatment of the patient. Since these instructions cannot possibly make provision for every turn the course of the disease will take under the influence of changing climatic conditions, they must of necessity be couched in general terms. As a result, they will contain prescriptions which do not meet a specific turn in the patient's condition in the way in which the doctor himself would deal with it if he were present. Yet in spite of that, the written instructions are absolutely binding upon the patient and he must follow them to the letter. The doctor, however, is not bound in this way: his mastery of medical science entitles him to change his manner of treatment as often as he sees fit, and he is not required to abide by the written instructions which he himself has given.

Similarly the statesman, because of his superior knowledge

24 303b.
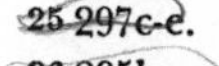
25 297c-e.
26 295b-e.

of political science, can enact any law he knows to be for the good of the governed, whether they consent to it or not. To meet a new situation, he may promulgate regulations which contravene what has formerly been enacted. The governed majority, who are ignorant of the art of ruling, have as little right to challenge the statesman's authority as the patient has to challenge the doctor's. In fact, just as the doctor may coerce his patient to submit to a certain course of treatment, so the statesman also has the right to use violence if necessary to enforce his laws. Accordingly, there is no need of laws as long as there is a kingly ruler who knows the science of statesmanship. But we can hardly expect that such a ruler will ever appear: "We must take things as they are, however, and kings do not arise in cities in the natural course of things in the way the royal bee is born in a beehive—one individual obviously outstanding in body and mind. And therefore it seems men have to gather together and work out written codes, chasing to catch the tracks of the true constitution." [27]

The laws which are thus laid down by and in the several existing states are not altogether bad. They embody the fruits of long experience, and before they were enacted an assembly of the people had to be persuaded that they were good and necessary. Therefore the laws must be obeyed, and any infringement of them must be forbidden and severely punished. They must be strictly enforced despite the fact that they do not really embody what is best and most just for each member of the community; being rigid, they cannot perfectly regulate the undulations and inconstancies of human life. Not to need any law at all under the dispensation of the true statesman would be the best state of affairs; but lacking that, the second-best alternative is to be governed by laws which must not be contravened.[28] It is a further indication of Plato's greater tolerance of human failings, of which we spoke above, that he makes allowance for introducing changes for the better in the code of laws, and that he actually states that individuals or

27 301d-e.
28 294b-300e.

groups who try to do so "are doing the same thing according to their lights as the true statesman." [29]

Plato goes even a step further in recognizing the importance of law. Though realizing that there is no state which is actually governed by a true royal statesman, and that, accordingly, any government here on earth is only an imitation of true government, he nevertheless accords to a law-abiding constitution the distinction of being a fairly close copy of the true government by the statesman.[30] It is the distinction between a law-abiding and a law-flouting constitution rather than the distinction between a government by consent and a government by violence, briefly hinted at but never seriously accepted,[31] which becomes the criterion for measuring the constitutions by which existing states are governed.[32] The rule of one man, if law-abiding, is called "monarchy"; if lawless, "tyranny." The lawful rule of a few men is an "aristocracy" and its opposite "oligarchy"; and finally, the rule of many is law-abiding or law-flouting "democracy." All these constitutions are, of course, inferior to the only true government, the rule of the royal statesman. But if a choice is to be made among them, Plato considers monarchy best and tyranny worst. Aristocracy and oligarchy occupy intermediate positions as the second best and second worst forms of government respectively, while democracy is the worst of the law-abiding but the best of the law-flouting constitutions, since, as the rule of the majority, "it is not capable of any real good or of any serious evil as compared with the other two." [33]

It is tempting to compare this classification with the discussion of the degenerate states in the *Republic*.[34] There the "aristocratic" state of the Guardians degenerates first into timocracy, then oligarchy (plutocracy), democracy, and finally tyranny. In both the *Republic* and the *Statesman* the arrange-

[29] 300d.

[30] 293e.

[31] 291d-292a; cf. also 276d-e.

[32] 300e-303b.

[33] 303a.

[34] *Republic* VIII-IX, 543a-576a.

ment of the scale of values and the distinction of the less bad from the more corrupt forms of government is determined by ideological rather than historical considerations. But whereas the scale in the *Republic* was determined by the ever-increasing encroachment of the appetites, especially of the lust for pleasure and the lust for power, upon the rational element, in the *Statesman,* one might almost say, the predominance of the appetites is taken for granted as inevitable in the actually existing states and, instead, the yardstick becomes adherence to the curbing power of the law. On this basis, several changes of the system adopted in the *Republic* are introduced. The most striking change is perhaps that the places of democracy and oligarchy are reversed in the scale of values: oligarchy is now presented as inferior to any kind of democracy, while democracy itself is divided into a law-abiding and a lawless kind. Here again we may detect evidence of a mellowing in Plato's attitude to people, which his contacts with the problems of government in Sicily had brought about. But there is another difference between the discussions of the degenerate states in the two dialogues which strikes much deeper. It comes out in a startling change in terminology: we observe that the name "aristocracy" is now no longer applied to the absolutely best government of the Guardians, but to a corporate kind of government by a group of the best people, which, however, comes only second after monarchy. The reasons for this are clear: the *Statesman* has relegated the government of the Guardians to the mythical era of Kronos and has elevated the philosopher-king of the *Republic* without his philosophy to the position of the desirable but probably unattainable ruler in the person of the true statesman. One might perhaps say that, in the *Republic,* the idea of the perfectibility of the state gives way to the idea of the perfectibility of the ruler. In the *Statesman,* on the other hand, the knowledge and insight of the ruler remain the ultimate criterion of good government, although, at the same time, there is greater skepticism about the possibility of ever attaining the perfect ruler. As a result, the distinction between the true statesman and the possibility of his actually arising is sharpened, and the rule of law is introduced as a second-best. But the rule of law is only grudgingly proposed in the *Statesman* as a concession to the weakness of human nature. It remained for the *Laws,* the last of Plato's works on political theory, to attribute to law a divine origin and to accept it fully as the only way in which good government can be established in human society.

THE DRAMATIC SETTING OF THE *STATESMAN*

It remains now to say a few words about the general setting of the dialogue and the persons who participate in it. The dramatic date of the *Statesman* is 399 B.C., shortly before the trial and death of Socrates. This is indicated at the end of the *Theaetetus,* with which, as we have shown above, the *Sophist* and the *Statesman* are directly connected in the narrative: Socrates tells us that he has to leave for the stoa of the King Archon to face the indictment which Meletus had brought against him.[1]

Theodorus of Cyrene, who also appears in the *Theaetetus* and in the *Sophist,* was a distinguished mathematician and allegedly a teacher of Plato and Theaetetus. We learn in the *Theaetetus* of his proof that the square roots of 3, 5, and the other non-square numbers up to 17 are irrational numbers.[2] He was a younger contemporary of Socrates, and must have been on friendly terms with him, as he introduces Theaetetus to Socrates in the *Theaetetus* and the Eleatic Stranger in the *Sophist.* The date of his birth is thought to be *ca.* 460 B.C.

The Eleatic Stranger, who appears only here and in the *Sophist,* remains nameless, presumably the better to embody the tradition of Parmenides (fl. *ca.* 450 B.C.) and Zeno (b. *ca.* 490 B.C.) of Elea in Lucania in Southern Italy. The main tenet of the school was the assertion of the unity of Being. The Stranger, though committed to that view, is not doctrinaire

[1] *Theaetetus* 210d.

[2] *Ibid.,* 147d-148b.

about it.[3] In general, he is depicted as a distinguished and respected visitor from abroad.

Young Socrates, or the Younger Socrates, as he is usually called, was a member of Plato's Academy. He was not related to his older and more famous namesake. He was a friend and fellow student of Theaetetus and became the teacher of Aristotle when the latter first came to Athens from Stagira as a seventeen-year-old boy.[4] We learn from Plato in the *Eleventh Epistle* of 360/59 B.C. that he or the Younger Socrates was invited to draft a code of laws for a colony that was to be founded by Laodamas of Thasos. The *Eleventh Epistle*, addressed to Laodamas, declines that invitation on the ground of Socrates' poor health and Plato's own advanced years. If we can take this as an indication of Socrates' interest in political science, it is all the more reason why he should be one of the chief participants in the *Statesman*.

MARTIN OSTWALD

[3] E.g., at *Sophist* 241d.

[4] See E. Kapp in *Philologus* 79 (1924), 223-233.

SYNOPSIS OF THE DIALOGUE

1. Introductory Conversation (257a-258a)

Socrates persuades the Eleatic Stranger, whom Theodorus has introduced to the company, to proceed to the definition of the statesman. Young Socrates is requested to act as respondent to the Stranger and agrees to do so.

2. The First Definition of the Statesman (258b-268d)

Statesmanship is an art. King, statesman, slavemaster, and master of the household are one in practicing it. It may well be practiced by an expert adviser not actually wielding political power but guiding the wielder of it. It is a theoretical art rather than a manual one, but it is "applied" and not "pure" like mathematical calculation. It gives orders on its own initiative and is one of the arts of the nurture of herds of living creatures. Immediate division of living creatures into men and animals is hasty and unphilosophical, like the popular division of men into Greeks and barbarians. Cranes might divide creatures into cranes and non-cranes. Statesmanship proves to be the art of the collective nurture of living creatures which are tame, live on the land, have no horns, do not interbreed with other creatures, walk on two legs, and have no feathers. Young Socrates is delighted with this result but the Stranger is not. The statesman is not all in all to his herd as the cowherd is. Many might dispute the "nurture" of the human herd—merchants, farmers, and doctors, for instance. We must therefore discover the flaw in our definition and correct it.

3. The Myth (268d-274d)

The folk stories of the age of Kronos and of the earthborn men, and the story of Atreus and Thyestes, are traces in the folk memory of cosmic changes which recur in great cycles. In the real "age of Kronos" a god takes personal charge of the universe and, through his assistant divine guardians, of the men and creatures in it. Life is supported without labor. There are no wars and no politics. Men and beasts share this paradise and are born in full maturity from the earth. They live from maturity to infancy in the opposite course to us and disappear in utmost infancy into the earth to be the seed of further generations of the earthborn. But we live in the so-called age of Zeus, which must persist until the universe, now revolving on its own initiative and increasingly forgetful of the divine guidance, comes so near to disruption and "the bottomless abyss of unlikeness" that the god takes pity and resumes control. He makes the universe "ageless and deathless" by his aid; it is neither of these in its own right.

4. The Revised Definition (274e-277a)

We can now see where our definition was wrong. We confused the statesman of the present era of the universe with the divine shepherd of mankind of the other era. Our statesmen are closer to their subjects in training and nurture than a shepherd can be to his flock, and we should have spoken of "concern for" herds, not "nurture of" herds. Furthermore, we made a confusion of king and tyrant by not marking off the voluntarily accepted tendance exercised by the former from the imposed tendance of the latter (this is later challenged, as far as the true statesman is concerned, at 292c). Statesmanship is therefore the art of tendance of the creatures previously defined when that tendance is voluntarily accepted by them. Young Socrates is satisfied with the definition thus revised, but the Stranger is not.

5. *The Nature of Example* (277a-279a)

Our definition is neither clear nor complete. We must seek the aid of an example. First of all, however, we must explain what an example is and show how it can be used. Children are helped to spell by recognizing letters and syllables of words they can already spell in words they cannot yet spell; likewise we may trace out the definition of a lesser-known concept by recognizing in it the same elements as are present in a better-known concept.

6. *The Definition of Weaving* (279a-283b)

The Stranger divines that the art of weaving woolen clothes will serve us as an example of statesmanship, and so he proceeds to a series of divisions in order to define this art. It must be distinguished from arts of manufacture of kindred fabrics, from separative arts, like the art of carding, which are parts of the general art of woolworking, and from merely subordinate arts whose products are nevertheless necessary to the weaver, such as the art of manufacturing shuttles. Only after distinguishing weaving explicitly from all of these can we claim to have defined it.

7. *Excess and Deficiency* (283b-287b)

Our detailed definition of weaving may be condemned as needlessly extended and the myth too may be criticized for being too long. Is this a fair complaint? We can only be sure if we know what excess and deficiency really are, and this implies possession of the art of measurement. But this art is twofold. One part of it is concerned with relative dimensions only, but another and a more important part of it is concerned with measurement in terms of the achievement of the due measure, the due time, and the due performance. This second art of measurement (which even philosophers fail to distinguish from the other) is vitally concerned in the operation of all the arts, so that their very existence depends upon it; and in examining dialectical method we shall have to have it always in mind and employ it. By this second art of measurement we must decide whether or not a discourse is too long. Does it achieve the "due performance" of making us better philosophers? If so, it is of the right length.

8. The Final Definition of the Statesman (287b-300e)

With the example of weaving to help us we may now proceed to define precisely the function of the statesman in the human political community. As there were subordinate arts which merely produced the tools which made weaving possible, so there are subordinate functions in the human community. These must be presumed if there is to be any society for the statesman to operate in and upon, but all these minor functions must be clearly distinguished from statesmanship itself. Three such classes of subordinate functionaries may be specified.

1. Primary producers of the physical requirements of the community. These requirements cannot be divided into less than seven classes—raw material at its first working, tools, vessels, carriages, seats, diversions, and nourishments.
2. Personal menial servants, day laborers, money-changers, merchants, venturers, and retail salesmen.
3. Clerks, heralds, soothsayers, and priests.

We must also distinguish the so-called statesmen who are in fact cheats and masters of illusion. Such are the rulers of our present states. We make much of the various "constitutions"—monarchy, oligarchy, democracy—in our political discussions, but none of them is a real constitution any more than those who rule in them are real statesmen. They are imitations and are counterfeit, and the true ruler and the true constitution must be distinguished from them.

For the true statesmanship, which alone makes the true constitution, is the practice of the art of ruling. When this art is at work, questions of compliance with laws, of consent in the ruled, and of wealth or poverty in the ruler do not arise. We do not question the professional status or the authority of a doctor because his remedies are unpalatable to us, and the true statesman is entitled to act with the same unfettered scientific authority. But such specialized political ability can never be widespread in any society. Neither an oligarchic clique nor an assembled multitude can possess it, though, as Young Socrates recalls, it may reside in an expert adviser on government not actually in executive authority himself.

Young Socrates is ready to accept all this except the statement that the true statesman may rule without laws. This is surely a hard saying.

The Stranger therefore invites him to consider the nature of law. It gives invariable commands which cannot be fitted to every situation or to every individual. Only the true statesman can, by the skillful use of his art, vary his control to meet the varying needs of the situation. A doctor would not bind himself to follow an earlier prescription rigidly if his patient's condition had changed. Law, however, is rigid and invariable. Even if it can be modified by persuading the people, such variations are not based on scientific insight, like that of the doctor who varies his prescription, or of the statesman who adopts a changed policy more salutary for society. No one who complains of such action as "violent" has any justification for his complaint. If there is no true statesman available, strict following of the law and punishment of all deviations from it is the best course, but legal tyranny over an art, and especially over the art of ruling, is intolerable. How could any art flourish if its principles were laid down as laws by a popular lay assembly, and if those who practiced it were answerable to that assembly? Difficult as life is now, a ban on the freedom of action and inquiry by those who practice an art would make life utterly unendurable.

Even so, complete absence of law or the violation of it without any insight into the true art of ruling is a further degradation. Where there is no statesmanship, let law be rigid. Law at its best attempts to copy the rules or prescriptions that a true statesman might issue, and it is entitled to the fullest authority in the absence of statesmanship—provided always that it abdicates where true statesmanship is present.

9. Digression on the Imitative Constitutions (300e-303b)

We ought perhaps to follow the expected paths of political discussion and consider the various so-called constitutions which seek to imitate the one true constitution. Monarchy, oligarchy, and democracy are each divisible into two, according as each abides by laws or flouts them—for in these "constitutions" the criterion of obedience to law does hold good. They may be classified thus:

Rule of One, if law-abiding, kingship; if flouting law, tyranny.
Rule of Few, if law-abiding, aristocracy; if flouting law, oligarchy.
Rule of Many, if law-abiding, democracy; if flouting law, still called democracy.

True statesmanship is a seventh constitution, to be distinguished from all these six as a god from men. If one has to decide which of the other six is hardest and which easiest to live under, the answer is that if all three are law-abiding, kingship is best, then aristocracy, then democracy. But if all three flout the law, democracy is best—or rather has least potency for evil—oligarchy is worse and tyranny worst of all. It is remarkable how our imperfect cities survive, but sometimes they make shipwreck as one would expect, and so they must until the one true statesman rules the one true commonwealth, not as a naturally superior being but as a truly just and wise man ruling impartially. Yet men prefer makeshifts, having little faith in the possibility of such a statesman.

10. Return to the Final Definition (303b-311c)

But we must return from imitators of the statesman to the statesman himself and we must now distinguish his function in society not from imitations of it but from the functions of those who are his genuine collaborators. These are orators, military leaders, and the judicature. Decision on the right occasion for war or for public justification of his policy must rest with the statesman himself. The orator's skill in public speaking and the military man's knowledge of strategy do not belong to the statesman as such but are to be at his service entirely and unquestionably, as and when required. Likewise, the statesman prescribes rules for the judicature and these must be the basis on which judgment is given in all disputes and particularly on those concerning mutual contractual obligations.

But we must now consider the nature of the statesman's weaving activity itself. Here we have to face a fundamental antinomy in human character which defies all that philosophers have said about the unity of virtue. Courage and moderation are principles at variance in human nature and set in opposition the men in whom they predominate. Nor is it a conflict of human temperament only; it becomes a political issue and states incline to aggressiveness or to appeasement as a set policy and in either case come to ruin.

The vigorous and aggressive are the warp of society, the quiet and moderate are the weft. The spinners and carders are the educators of the young. By testing the children in games and then in formal instruction they must provide the statesman with thread strong enough to stand up to the strains of the weaving process but not recalcitrant to the discipline which shapes all who enter into the fabric of society. Those who cannot pass this test may be degraded into slavery.

All fit material taken over from the educators the statesman will use to weave the web of state. The supreme art is to blend warp and weft, the courageous and the moderate. This will be achieved by linking all the citizens by causing them to share the same ideals and to cherish the same ultimate values. But this divine link will call for human ties also, and these the statesman must seek to forge. Marriage must not be, as it is now, for money, nor may like characters be permitted to mate, for this leads to excess of character in one direction or another. Warplike strength must be mated with weftlike moderation. Magistracies, too, must combine both types. Thus, harmonious fellowship will be wrought out of this supreme work of the royal weaver who is the true statesman.

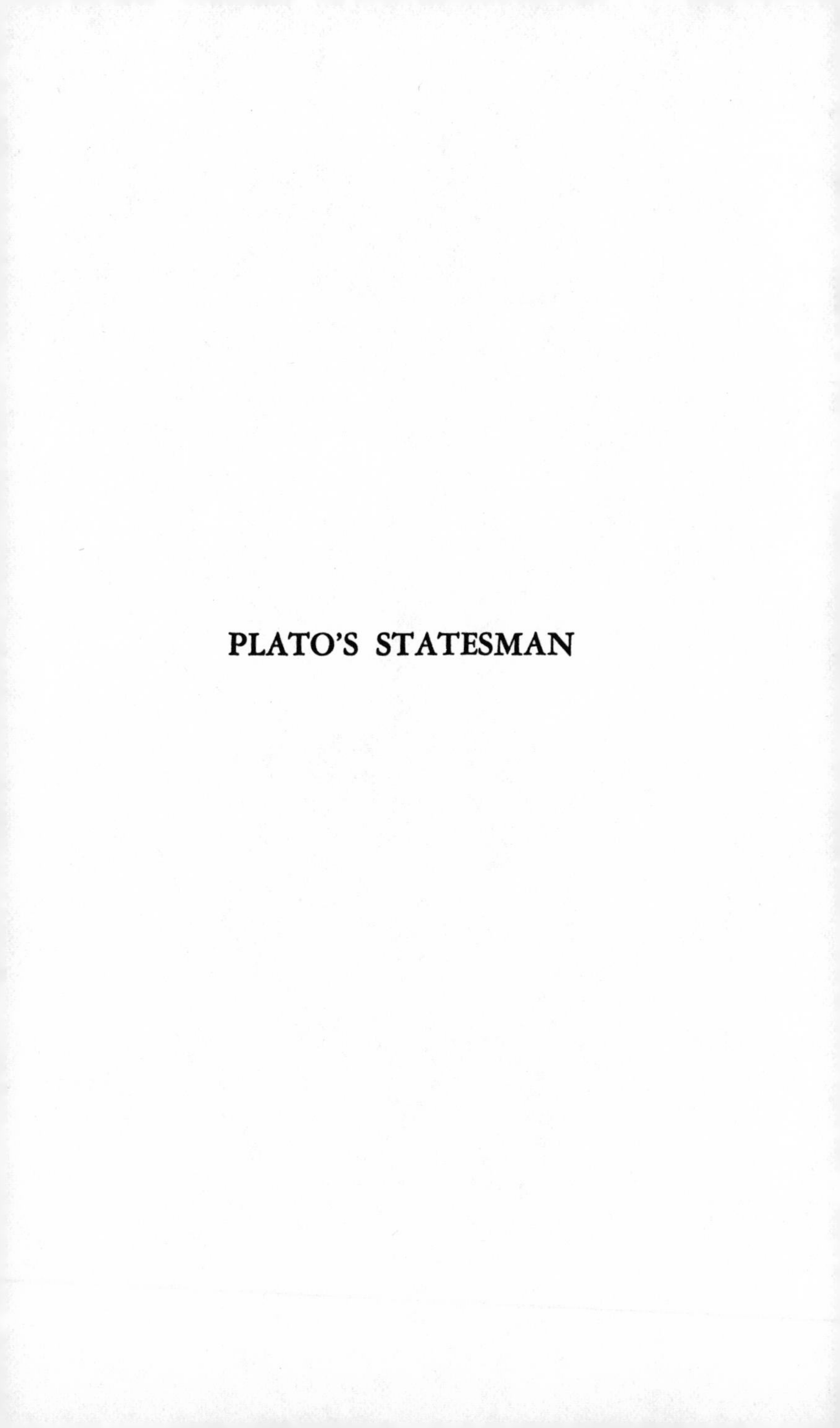

PLATO'S STATESMAN

STATESMAN

CHARACTERS OF THE DIALOGUE

SOCRATES	THEODORUS
STRANGER FROM ELEA	YOUNG SOCRATES

1. Introductory Conversation (257a-258a)

Socr. Theodorus, I am really very much indebted to you for my introduction to Theaetetus and to our guest from Elea. 257

Theo. Good, but you are likely to be three times as much in my debt, Socrates, when they have done their task and defined the statesman and the philosopher, in addition to the sophist, for you.

Socr. Three times as much? Really, my dear Theodorus, must it go on record that we heard our greatest mathematician and geometer say that?

Theo. What do you mean, Socrates? b

Socr. Are we to say that we heard you reckoning all these three as of equal value when their real values differ to an extent that defies all your mathematical expressions of proportion?

Theo. By Ammon, god of my native Libya, well said, Socrates, and a fair hit! Your dropping on my blunder in calculation like this shows that you have really remembered your mathematics! But I will have my revenge for this some other time. Now, Sir, we turn to you. Please do not tire of favoring us with your assistance but go on with your discussion of the statesman or the philosopher, whichever you prefer to define c first.

Str. Yes, we must do that, Theodorus. We have set ourselves to the task and now we must not withdraw from it till all our definitions are complete. But we must also consider Theaetetus here—what ought I to do about him?

Theo. In what way?

Str. Shall we give him a rest from philosophic wrestling and take on his fellow gymnast, the young Socrates, in his place—or have you any other suggestion?

Theo. No, take on young Socrates this time, as you suggest. They are both young and will be better able to carry through stiff exercise by being rested in turn.

d *Socr.* Furthermore, Sir, they might both be said to have some sort of kinship with me. Theaetetus, according to you, is like me in facial looks and Socrates bears the same name.
258 Sharing a name entails kinship in some sense, and, of course, we ought always to seize opportunities of discovering those who may be our kinfolk by conversing with them. Yesterday I joined in discussion with Theaetetus; today I have listened to him answering you. I have not heard Socrates speak either in discussion or in reply. He too must be tested,[1] so he shall reply to me another time, but for the present let him answer you.

Str. Very good! Socrates, you hear what Socrates says?

Y.S. Yes.

Str. Do you agree to his proposal?

Y.S. Yes, certainly.

2. *The First Definition of the Statesman* (258b-268d)

b *Str.* Evidently you are putting no obstacles in the way of our advance, and I think I am still less entitled to do so. Well, then, after finding the sophist, the task we now have to face together, it seems to me, is to search out the statesman. Tell me, then, Socrates, whether he too must be classified as one of those who possess some kind of expert knowledge, or must we begin with some other kind of definition?

Y.S. No, he is to be defined as a kind of expert.

[1] Or "have his share in the inquiry."

Str. Well, then, must we distinguish the forms of knowledge as we did when looking for his predecessor?

Y.S. It would seem so.

Str. But the line of division required now appears to differ from the previous one, Socrates.

Y.S. What then?

Str. It follows another division. c

Y.S. It may well be so.

Str. Where shall a man find the way of the statesman then? For we must track out and distinguish this path from all the rest by setting upon it the seal of its distinctive form. All roads divergent from it we must mark out also as one common class. Thus we must bring our minds to conceive of all forms of knowledge as falling under one or the other of these two classes: statecraft and knowledge other than statecraft.

Y.S. This must be your task, Sir. It is not for me to attempt it.

Str. Yes, but it must be your achievement as well, Socrates, d when all becomes clear to us both.

Y.S. Very well.

Str. Then consider the science of number and certain other sciences closely akin to it. Are they not unconcerned with any form of practical activity, yielding us pure knowledge only?

Y.S. That is the case.

Str. But it is quite otherwise with carpentry and manufacture in general. These possess science embodied as it were in a practical activity and inseparable from it. Their products do not exist before the arts come into operation and their operation is an integral part of the emergence of the product e from its unworked state.

Y.S. True. What of it?

Str. You must use this distinction to divide the totality of sciences into two classes: name the one "applied," the other "pure."

Y.S. I agree. Let your distinction be drawn, and let all science, which is one whole, be divided into these two parts.

Str. Are we then to regard the statesman, the king, the slavemaster, and the master of a household as essentially one though we use all these names for them, or shall we say that four distinct sciences exist, each of them corresponding to one of the four titles? But let me put this in another way easier to follow.

Y.S. And what is that?

259 *Str.* I will tell you. Suppose we find a medical man who is not himself practicing as a public medical officer but who nevertheless is competent to advise a doctor actually serving in that capacity. Must not the expert knowledge the adviser possesses be described by the same title as that of the functionary whom he is advising?

Y.S. Yes.

Str. Well, then, consider a man who, though himself a private citizen, is capable of giving expert advice to the ruler of a country. Shall we not say that he possesses the same science as the ruler himself ought to possess?

Y.S. We shall indeed say so.

b *Str.* But the science possessed by the true king is the science of kingship?

Y.S. Yes.

Str. The possessor of this science then, whether he is in fact in power or has only the status of a private citizen, will properly be called "royal," since his knowledge of the art qualifies him for the title whatever his circumstances.

Y.S. Yes, he is undoubtedly entitled to that name.

Str. Then consider a further point. The slavemaster and the master of a household are identical.

Y.S. Yes.

Str. Furthermore, is there much difference between a large household organization and a small-sized city, so far as the exercise of authority over it is concerned?

Y.S. None.

c *Str.* Well, then, our point is clearly made. One science covers all these several spheres and we will not quarrel with a man who prefers any one of the particular names for it; he can call it royal science, political science, or science of household management.

Y.S. It makes no difference.

Str. Now comes another obvious point. What a king can do to maintain his rule by using his hands or his bodily faculties as a whole is very slight in comparison with what he can do by mental power and force of personality.

Y.S. Manifestly.

Str. So a king's art is closer to theoretic knowledge than to manual work or indeed to practical work in general? d

Y.S. Yes.

Str. You agree then that we may group together under one term statesmanship and the statesman, and kingship and the king, since they are all identical in force?

Y.S. Certainly.

Str. Let us go on to the next stage and see if we can proceed to a division of the kinds of theoretic knowledge.

Y.S. Good.

Str. Look attentively then and see if we cannot discover a natural partition within such knowledge.

Y.S. Tell me what kind of partition.

Str. The following: there exists, we agree, an art of counting. e

Y.S. Yes.

Str. That belongs quite definitely to the class of theoretic sciences, I presume.

Y.S. Of course.

Str. Now when the art of counting has ascertained a numerical difference we do not assign it any further task save that of pronouncing on what has been ascertained, do we?

Y.S. No.

Str. Now consider a master builder. No master builder is a manual worker—he directs the work of others.

Y.S. Yes.

Str. He provides the knowledge but not the manual labor.

Y.S. True.

Str. So he might fairly be said to share in theoretic science. 260

Y.S. He might indeed.

Str. But it is characteristic of him that when he has delivered a verdict on the facts he has not ended his task in the way the calculator has. The master builder must give the appropriate directions to each of the workmen until they complete the work assigned.

Y.S. That is so.

Str. Therefore all such sciences are quite as "theoretical" as calculation and its kindred sciences are, but the two groups differ from one another in that the one is content to give a b verdict, but the other issues a command for performance of further actions.

Y.S. This is clearly the difference between them.

Str. Well, then, may we claim that it is a sound division to split the whole of theoretical science into two parts and to call one directive and the other critical?

Y.S. Yes—I for one would agree to it.

Str. I hope so, for it is desirable that those sharing a task should be of one mind.

Y.S. Indeed it is.

Str. So long as we ourselves share this happy agreement we must not bother about the opinions of the rest of the world.

Y.S. Yes.

c *Str.* Well, then, in which of these groups of sciences do we find a place for the king? In the critical class—as though he were a mere spectator of truth? Is he not rather in the other, directive class? Does not his position in control of men imply this?

Y.S. Of course he is in the second group.

Str. Good, but we must now look further at the directive class and see if we find a division in it somewhere. I think I have lighted on one. There is a difference between kings and d heralds analogous to the difference between the art of the producer-salesman and that of the retailer.

Y.S. How so?

Str. Retailers take over what someone else has made and then sell a second time what was first sold to them.

Y.S. Quite so.

Str. Similarly, heralds receive commands which have been thought out and issued by someone else; then they issue them at second hand to others.

Y.S. Very true.

Str. Well, then, are we going to confound the science of kingship with the science of the interpreter, the coxswain, the prophet, or the herald, or with any of this large group of kindred sciences, simply because all of them are concerned (as admittedly they are) with issuing orders? We thought out an analogy just now: can we not think out a name as well, seeing that unfortunately there is no normal description of the general class of "givers of firsthand orders"? We will make the division at this point and name a "predirective" science into which we will put the race of kings. The other class we can completely neglect, leaving it to someone else to invent a further common name for what it covers. It is for the king we are searching, not for his opposite. e 261

Y.S. Exactly.

Str. Well, then, his group has been fairly distinguished from the others, the decisive factor being that the kingly group issues its own commands while the other group merely passes commands on. Now we must subdivide the kingly group if we find it susceptible of a division.

Y.S. We must look for one.

Str. Yes, and I think I have found one. Keep close to me and share the work of dividing.

Y.S. Where is the division?

Str. Take any ruler we may observe at his work of issuing orders. Is not the purpose of his action the production of something? b

Y.S. Of course.

Str. Moreover, as for products in general, they are easily divided into two classes.

Y.S. How?

Str. Considering them as a whole we find some lifeless, the rest alive.

Y.S. Yes.

Str. By this distinction we can divide, if we wish to do so, the directive group of theoretic sciences.

Y.S. Along what line?

Str. We assign one section to superintendence of the production of lifeless things, the other to superintendence of the c production of living things. This effects an exhaustive division of the group.

Y.S. Yes, it does.

Str. Let us put aside the one section and, taking the other as our unit, divide it into two.

Y.S. Which of the two sections do you suggest that we take for subdivision?

Str. Surely the section concerned with the issue of directives about living creatures. It goes without saying that the king is never concerned with directives concerning lifeless things in the way the master builder is. Kingship is a nobler thing: it d works among living creatures and its power extends to these alone.

Y.S. True.

Str. Now the breeding and nurturing of living creatures can be seen to be of two kinds. They may either be reared singly or in flocks collectively.

Y.S. They may.

Str. But we shall certainly not find the statesman to be a man who rears one creature, like some cowman or groom. He is much more like the man in charge of a herd of cows or of a stud of horses.

Y.S. That is quite clear, once it is put as you have put it now.

e *Str.* How shall we describe the section of the art of rearing living things which has to do with rearing them collectively? Shall we call it "herd nurture" or "collective nurture"?

Y.S. We can use whichever name better helps our argument.

Str. Excellently said, Socrates. If you hold fast to this principle of avoiding contention over names you will turn out to be rich with an ever greater store of wisdom as you approach old age. We will apply this sound principle to the present case and do as you bid me. Do you see how we can divide the nurture of herds into twin sections, so as to cordon off the object of our search in one of them and leave him an area only 262 half the size of the one he is free to roam in at present?

Y.S. I will try my hardest to cordon him off. I think the division is to be made between nurture of men and nurture of beasts.

Str. You certainly made the division most promptly and bravely; but I think we must not let this happen again if we can help it.

Y.S. Let what happen again?

Str. We must beware lest we break off one small fragment of a class and then contrast it with the many important sections left behind. We must only divide where there is a real b cleavage between specific forms. The section must always possess a specific form.[2] It is splendid if one really can divide off the class sought for immediately from all the rest—that is, if such immediate division is correctly made. You had such direct tactics in mind just now and hastened the argument to its conclusion. You saw that our search led us to men, and so you thought you had found the real division. But it is dangerous, Socrates, to chop reality up into small portions. It is always safer to go down the middle to make our cuts: we are more likely to find the specific form in this way; and that makes all the difference in an investigation. c

Y.S. What do you mean, Sir?

Str. I will try to be still clearer, Socrates, for you are the kind of person it is a pleasure to teach. A fully satisfactory demonstration is not possible now, circumstances being what

[2] It is hardly possible to be more precise than Plato himself in the use of the terms "class," "species," etc. γένος (class) is sometimes used with a wider connotation than εἶδος (specific form), sometimes it is virtually identical in meaning. μέρος (part, section, portion) is carefully distinguished from εἶδος at 263b, and yet at 279b Plato chooses μέρος rather than εἶδος to speak of the divisions into species concerned with weaving. Of course a μέρος *can* be an εἶδος and so this is not inconsistent; but it is remarkable evidence of Plato's avoidance of technical terms.

they are, but we must try for the sake of clearness to push the explanation a little further.

Y.S. Thank you, but what kind of mistake do you say that we made in our division just now?

Str. The kind of mistake a man would make who, seeking to d divide the class of human beings into two, divided them into Greeks and barbarians. This is a division most people in this part of the world make. They separate the Greeks from all other nations, assuming that they are a class apart, and they group all other nations together as a class, ignoring the fact that it is an indeterminate class made up of peoples who have no intercourse with each other and speak different languages. Lumping all this non-Greek residue together, they think it must constitute one real class because they have a common name, "barbarian," to attach to it. Take another example. A man might think that he was dividing number into two specific forms if he cut off the number 10,000 from all others and e set it apart as one specific form. He might go on to invent a single name for the whole of the rest of number, and then claim that because it possessed the invented common name it was in fact the other true class of number—"number other than 10,000." Surely it would be better and closer to the real structure of the specific forms to make a central division of number into odd and even or of humankind into male and female. A division which splits Lydians or Phrygians or any other peoples off and arrays them against all the rest can only be made when a man fails to arrive at a true division into two groups each of which, after separation, is not only a portion 263 but also a real class.

Y.S. Quite so, Sir, but this is just the difficulty. How can one learn to distinguish more clearly between a mere portion and a class, and recognize them as being really different?

Str. My dear Socrates, this is no light order. We have already strayed rather too far from the argument set as our task, and here you are asking that we stray still further! For the moment let us go back to the argument, as is only right. We b will get on the track of your problem some other time when we are free to do so and then we will follow it out to the end. But there is one caution I will add here. Do not suppose that in what I say now I have given you a full explanation of the principle.

Y.S. What principle do you mean?

Str. The principle that a portion and a specific form are not identical.

Y.S. Can you be more explicit?

Str. Where a true specific form is established, it must necessarily also be a portion of the total class of which it is declared a specific form. But the converse is not true, since a portion is not necessarily a specific form. You can claim my authority, Socrates, for asserting this and for denying the contrary.

Y.S. That I shall do.

Str. Good! Now help me to settle the next question. c

Y.S. What is that?

Str. Consider what caused us to stray from the argument and brought us to this point. I think that the trouble began at the moment when you were asked how we were to divide the science of tending herds and you answered with alacrity that there are two classes of living creature, one of them being mankind, and the other the rest of the animals lumped together.

Y.S. True.

Str. It became clear to me then that you were breaking off a mere portion, and that because you were able to give the common name "animals" to what was left—namely, to all creatures other than man—you thought that these creatures do in actual fact make up one class. d

Y.S. Yes, that was so.

Str. But, my gallant young friend, look at it this way. This kind of classification might be undertaken by any other creature capable of rational thought—for instance, cranes[3] are re-

[3] Aristotle (*Hist. An.*, 488a, 12, also 614b, 18) says that "there are many signs of intelligent behavior in cranes." The crane was both gregarious and "political," with a recognized leader. On their autumn migration

puted to be rational and there may be others. They might invest themselves with a unique and proper dignity and classify the race of cranes as being distinct from all other creatures; the rest they might well lump together, men included, giving them the common appellation of "the beasts." So let us try to e be on the watch against mistakes of that kind.

Y.S. How can we avoid them?

Str. By not attempting too general a division of the class of living creatures. We shall then be less liable to such errors.

Y.S. Yes, we must not do that.

Str. And it was here our mistake was made just now.

Y.S. What precisely was it?

Str. The directive portion of theoretic science, in so far as it directs the rearing of living creatures, was our concern, but we added "the rearing of them in herds." That is so, is it not?

Y.S. Yes.

264 *Str.* This last element of the definition, "rearing in herds," implied a prior division of all living creatures according to wildness and tameness. Those amenable to training and control we call tame animals, those which are not, wild animals.

Y.S. True.

Str. Now the science we are hunting down has always been and still is one that works among tame creatures; furthermore, it is to be looked for among tame creatures which are gregarious.

Y.S. Yes.

Str. Let us avoid making divisions in the way we did just now, in a desperate hurry and with our attention fixed only on the whole class. Only thus shall we reach the statesman's b art in good time. It has already landed us in the situation the proverb warns us against!

Y.S. Which proverb is this?

---

they maintained a strict formation which could be interpreted as a triangle or as the letter Δ implying mathematical or grammatical wisdom (Aristotle, fr. 342, Rose; see also Cicero, *De nat. deorum* II, 49, Plutarch, *Moralia,* 967c, 979a, and Aelian, *De nat. an.,* III, 13).

Str. "More haste" in our work of correct division has meant "less speed" for us.

Y.S. But it has been a happy mischance, Sir.

Str. That may be so, but now let us try again from the beginning to divide the science of collective rearing. It may well be that the argument itself as we proceed with it will show you more clearly the very thing you are so eager to discover. Answer me this.

Y.S. What?

Str. I want to know if you happen to have heard people speak of something you can hardly have seen for yourself—herds of tame fishes. I know you have not been to see them in c the aquariums in the Nile or in the Great King's ponds. But you might possibly have seen such fishes in ornamental fountains yourself.

Y.S. Of course I have seen them, and I have heard many people speak of the others.

Str. It is the same with the flocks of tame cranes and tame geese in Thessaly—even though you have never toured the Thessalian Plains you have at least heard of them and you believe that such flocks exist.

Y.S. Yes, of course.

Str. My reason for asking you all this is to show that crea- d tures reared in herds may be of two kinds: some live in water, others live on land.

Y.S. Yes, I agree.

Str. Do you also agree, then, that we have to divide the science of herd rearing on this principle into two sections? May we assign to each of these its part and call the one "water-herd rearing," the other "land-herd rearing"?

Y.S. Again, I agree.

Str. One need hardly ask to which of these sciences the kingly art belongs—the answer is obvious. e

Y.S. Of course.

Str. The next division of the land-herd-rearing section of herd rearing can be made by anyone.

Y.S. How?

Str. By dividing it between walkers and flyers.

Y.S. Oh yes, of course.

Str. Well, then, is not the statesman's art to be sought among the arts dealing with walking herds? Do you not think that, as they say, even the most witless would judge this to be so?

Y.S. Yes, I do.

Str. Then we must effect a division of walking-herd tendance into two parts, just as we recently divided number into two.

Y.S. Clearly.

265 *Str.* But see what has happened. We see two paths lying before us inviting us to the goal toward which our argument has progressed. One path reaches the goal quicker but divides off a small class from a large one. The other is a longer way round but it observes the principle we enunciated before that we should always divide down the middle where possible. We can go on by whichever of these paths we prefer.

Y.S. Is it impossible to take them both?

Str. To take both at once is impossible—that is an amazing suggestion, Socrates! But obviously we can take them in turn.

b *Y.S.* Then I vote for taking them in turn.

Str. That is easy, for there is not much further to go. At the outset or halfway your command would have been difficult for us to obey, but now, since you desire it, let us take the longer path first: we shall get to its end more easily now while we are fresher. See this division then.

Y.S. Tell me what it is.

Str. We find a division of tame, herded, walking creatures ready-made in nature.

Y.S. What is it?

Str. Some grow horns, the rest do not.

c *Y.S.* That is evident.

Str. Divide then the science of rearing walking herds into two portions, assigning each its sphere; but use a general definition in doing so. For if you are anxious about naming each, the business will be complicated needlessly.

Y.S. How shall we state the matter then?

Str. We will say this. The science of rearing walking herds has been divided into two: the one section of it is assigned to rearing horned herds, and the other to rearing hornless herds.

Y.S. The division shall stand, in these terms. In any case **d** there can be no further question about it.

Str. See now, our king stands out clearly once more: he is shepherd of a hornless herd.

Y.S. Unmistakably so!

Str. Let us break up this herd into its component parts then, and try to assign to the king the place really belonging to him.

Y.S. By all means.

Str. Where shall we divide it? By distinguishing whole-hoof and cloven-hoof, or interbreeding and non-interbreeding? Which do you prefer? You understand what I mean, I suppose?

Y.S. What?

Str. You know that horses and asses are capable of inter- **e** breeding.

Y.S. Yes.

Str. But all other tame, hornless herds are incapable of interbreeding.

Y.S. Of course.

Str. What of the statesman, then? Is the herd he has in his charge capable of interbreeding with another or incapable?

Y.S. Incapable, of course.

Str. This group we must now divide again into two as before, it would seem.

Y.S. Yes, we must.

Str. But the class of tame, gregarious living creatures has 266 already been reduced to its component elements save for the division of two of these from each other. For dogs cannot claim to be counted in the class of gregarious animals.

Y.S. No, they cannot, but by what means are we to separate the remaining pair?

Str. By a method very appropriate for application by Theaetetus and yourself, seeing that both of you are geometers.

Y.S. What is that?

Str. I would say, "By the diagonal, and secondly by the diagonal of the diagonal."

Y.S. What do you mean?

b *Str.* What do you say of our human constitution? How is this human race of ours endowed? So far as its walking potential is concerned, is it not very like the diagonal? Has it not the power of two feet?

Y.S. So it has.

Str. Moreover the character of the remaining component of the class is in turn of the power possessed by the diagonal of our human diagonal, since its native walking potential is one of two feet twice over.

Y.S. Of course it is, and I think I see what you are meaning to say.[4]

[4] Here the reader is likely to be more in doubt than young Socrates concerning the meaning. The joke is somewhat heavy and professorial but it is no doubt meant to amuse Theodorus, who is in the background and may well be bored by the divisions. It is evidence that the Stranger, like Socrates, has not forgotten his geometry. At *Theaetetus,* 147d, e the young Theaetetus reports the teaching he has received from Theodorus on δυνάμεις οὐ σύμμετροι, "surds" or irrational numbers represented by incommensurable lines geometrically. Theaetetus says that he has just been discussing these matters with the young Socrates. The Stranger's pleasantry is therefore a tribute to Theodorus and to the young Socrates and is not quite as irrelevant as it appears.

The following diagram should make the point clear:

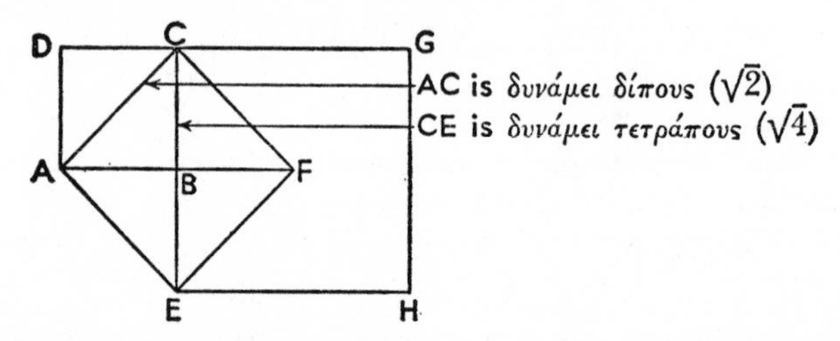

Let ABCD be a square whose sides are 1 foot, and which therefore is 1 sq. ft. in area. Then the diagonal AC is $\sqrt{2}$ feet in length (by "Pythagoras' theorem" since $(AC)^2 = (AD)^2 + (DC)^2 = 1^2 + 1^2 = 1$ sq. ft. + 1 sq. ft. = 2 sq. ft.). Then the square AEFC has sides of $\sqrt{2}$ feet and an

Str. Good! Now here is another conclusion which we have reached by our divisions which is good for laughs. Do we see it, Socrates? c

Y.S. What is it?

Str. This human family of ours has turned out to be in one class with and a running mate of the most noble and the most lazy of all the creatures.[5]

Y.S. Yes, I see. What a funny coincidence!

Str. Still, isn't it reasonable after all that the slowest should be the last to arrive?

Y.S. Yes, of course you're right.

Str. But there is another thing to notice. What a funny situation the king is in! He has kept pace with his herd and so

---

area of 2 sq. ft. But CBE, the diagonal of this square AEFC, has as its square the sum of the squares on its sides AC, AE, that is $2 + 2 = 4$ sq. ft. CBE is therefore $\sqrt{4}$ feet in length. So AC is "potentially two feet," CE "potentially four feet" in the sense that they are the sides of squares of 2 sq. ft. (ACFE) and 4 sq. ft. (ECGH) respectively. But AC is also the "diameter" (of the unit foot square) and CE is the "diameter of the diameter" in that it is the "diameter" of the square AEFC whose side AC is itself the "diameter" of the square ABCD. The Greeks used "diameter" for "diagonal" in our usage.

The play is of course upon πούς, which means both "foot" in the physical and in the mathematical sense, and also upon δύναμις—which means both "power," "potency," and "square root." Man (potentially two-footed) : pig (potentially four-footed) : : AC : CE.

[5] The exact meaning of this passage and the exchange following it escapes us, because Plato does not specify what creature he means. Some scholars believe that a new division of bipeds into men and birds is introduced here. In that case, "noble" must be taken seriously, and what is here translated as "lazy" must be rendered as "dexterous," another possible meaning of the adjective Plato employs here. However, this would make the funniness of the situation hard to see. Others think that "noble" is used facetiously and that pigs are classed together with humans as tame, gregarious, walking, hornless, and non-interbreeding animals. Justification for that view is sought in the use of *hystata* ("last") which may be a pun on *hys* ("pig"), and by the fact that in the *Theaetetus* (161c) the arbitrariness of Protagoras' famous dictum is ludicrously challenged by "Pig is the measure of all things." As this would explain the funny situation, the latter interpretation has been adopted here. [Ed.]

d he has been running a race with the man who is of all men best trained for living a lazy life.

Y.S. Yes, just so.

Str. This is a still clearer illustration, Socrates, of the principle we laid down in our inquiry concerning the sophist.

Y.S. What was that?

Str. That in a philosophical search for a definition (like the present one) the presence or absence of dignity in the object under definition is irrelevant. Lowly and exalted must receive equal consideration and the search must proceed in its own way to reach the truest conclusion obtainable.

Y.S. That seems to be right.

Str. Well, now, am I to lead you, without waiting for you to e ask me, along the shorter of the roads which we discovered as leading to the definition of the king?

Y.S. Do so, please.

Str. In my opinion, then, we should have started by dividing land creatures into a two-footed and a four-footed class. We then see the human race sharing the lot of being a two-footed herd with the winged tribes and none else. Next, we divide the bipeds into winged and wingless. After this division the science of shepherding mankind will have been brought to light. Now we must bring our statesman and king and set him over this herd like a charioteer, and hand over to him the reins of the state; for they belong to him and his alone is this science of government.

267 *Y.S.* Your debt to me is nobly discharged by the definition you have made—and you have more than paid it, for you have thrown in the digression by way of interest.

Str. Come, then, let us gather up the threads of our argument and work out from start to finish our definition of what is called "political science."

Y.S. Let us do so by all means.

Str. We made a first division of theoretic science by taking the directive part of it. Of this we took the part which we described by analogy with the producer-salesman as "predirective." From this predirective science we split off that which directs the rearing of living things, a very important class of the whole. Animal rearing was divided and we chose out of it rearing in herds and, next, rearing of herds that live on land. Dividing this again, we chose the art of rearing hornless creatures. We then took a part of this and, if one must coin for it one single name, it will be a compound three words long—"non-interbreeding-herd-tendance." As for the further divisions, only the portion of "man-tendance" is left in the two-footed herd—and so we reach the object of our search, namely, statesmanship or kingship (which is another name for statesmanship). b c

Y.S. Yes, we really have reached our conclusion.

Str. Do you really think so, Socrates? Do you think our task as complete as you make out?

Y.S. Why do you ask?

Str. Have we dealt fully with the problem we were given to solve? Is there not a shortcoming and a very grave one in our treatment of it, the shortcoming of arriving at some kind of definition of a king but failing to work through to a really complete and adequate definition? d

Y.S. What do you mean?

Str. I will try to make my meaning clearer—to myself as well as to you.

Y.S. Do so, please.

Str. We found just now many arts of herd-tendance of which statesmanship is one particular instance. Statesmanship is in charge of the rearing of one particular kind of herd.

Y.S. Yes.

Str. Our argument defined it as the science of the collective rearing of men—as distinct from the rearing of horses or other animals.

Y.S. Quite so.

Str. But we have to notice one respect in which a king differs from all other herdsmen. e

Y.S. What is that?

Str. Do we find any other herdsman challenged by a rival who practices another art and yet claims that he shares with the herdsman the duty of feeding the herd?

Y.S. How do you mean?

Str. You see how merchants, farmers, and all who prepare the grain for food—yes, and teachers of gymnastics and doctors as well—would all dispute the title "keepers of mankind" with the herdsman we have called "statesman." These others would 268 all contend that they are in charge of rearing mankind—and of feeding the leaders themselves as well as the mass of the human herd.

Y.S. Would they not be quite right?

Str. Maybe. We will examine this point further, but we can say at once with certainty that no one disputes a cowherd's position in any of these matters. He feeds his herd himself, and he is also its doctor. He is its matchmaker, too, one might say, and none but he understands the midwife's duties when b confinements occur and babies have to be brought into the world. Furthermore, in so far as his charges feel a natural need for games and music, who is so good as to cheer them, who so gifted to charm and soothe them? For he is master of the music best suited to his herd, whether he plays it on the pipes or sings unaccompanied. And so it is in the case of every other herdsman, is it not?

Y.S. Certainly it is.

Str. How then can the definition of the king reached in our discussion show up as correct and flawless in the light of these c new facts? We are claiming that he alone is herdsman and keeper of the human flock, but we are merely singling him out as such from a host of competitors.

Y.S. Certainly this will not do.

Str. Then we were quite right to feel anxious a little while ago when the suspicion came over us that, though the figure we described might be a kingly one, we had not yet achieved a real portrait of the statesman. For we cannot reveal him finally in his proper quality till we have removed and put apart from him the throng of rivals that crowd around him and claim to share his herdsmanship.

Y.S. Yes, we were quite right. d

Str. So we must aim at a complete description, Socrates, unless we are to bring disgrace on our argument in the end.

Y.S. Yes, we must avoid that at all costs.

3. The Myth (268d-274d)

Str. Then we must begin all over again from another starting point and travel by another road.

Y.S. What kind of road must this be?

Str. We may perhaps bring in some pleasant stories. There is a celebrated legend a large part of which we must now use for our purposes; after that we must go on as before, dividing always and choosing one part only, until we arrive at the e summit of our climb and the object of our journey. Shall we begin?

Y.S. Yes, certainly.

Str. Come then, listen closely to my story as a child would. After all, you are not so very many years too old for stories.

Y.S. Do continue, please.

Str. Many of these old stories have happened before and will happen again. Among them is the one about the portent that occurred in the famous quarrel between Atreus and Thyestes. I expect you have heard the story and remember what they say happened at that time.

Y.S. You refer, I suppose, to the strange sign of the golden lamb.[6]

[6] Myrtilus, son of Hermes, had assisted Pelops to secure the hand of Hippodamia; but Pelops subsequently cast Myrtilus into the sea out of jealousy. Then Hermes caused a golden lamb to grow among the flocks of Atreus (son of Pelops). The possession of this lamb carried with it the right to rule in Mycenae. Strife was thus caused between Atreus and his brother Thyestes. Thyestes debauched Aerope, wife of Atreus, persuaded her to give him the lamb and seized the kingdom. But Zeus, to vindicate

269 *Str.* Oh no, not to that, but to the change in the rising and setting of the sun and the other stars. The story tells us that on this occasion these all set where they now rise and rose where they now set. Afterwards, however, when he had testified by this miracle to the justice of Atreus' claims, the god restored all these heavenly bodies to their present system of motion.

Y.S. Yes, that comes into the story too.

Str. Then again, we have heard of the reign of Kronos from many storytellers.

b *Y.S.* From most of them, I should say.

Str. Yes, and what else? Are we not told that men of that former age were earthborn and not born of human parents?

Y.S. That is also one of the old stories.

Str. All these stories originate from the same event, and so do hosts of others yet more marvelous than these. However, as this great event took place so long ago, some of them have faded from man's memory; others survive, but they have become scattered and have come to be told in a way which obscures their real connection with one another. No one has related the great event which is the origin of all of them; it is c this event which we must now recount. Once it has been related, its relevance to our present demonstration of the nature of a king will become apparent.

Y.S. Excellent. Please go on, and leave nothing unsaid.

Str. Listen then. There is an era in which the god himself assists the universe on its way and helps it in its rotation. There is also an era in which he releases his control. He does this when its circuits have completed the due limit of the time thereto appointed. Thereupon it begins to revolve in the contrary sense under its own impulse—for it is a living creature d and has been endowed with reason by him who framed it in

---

Atreus' claim to the throne, caused the sun and the Pleiades to change their courses. The portent had its effect and the throne was restored to Atreus. This form of the story was followed by Euripides in his *Orestes* (988 ff.) and is adopted by Plato here.

the beginning. Now this capacity for rotation in reverse is of necessity native to it for a reason I must tell.

Y.S. What is that reason?

Str. Ever to be the same, steadfast and abiding, is the prerogative of the divinest of things only. The nature of the bodily does not entitle it to this rank. Now the heaven, or the universe as we have chosen to call it, has received many blessed gifts from him who brought it into being, but it has also been made to partake of bodily form. Hence it is impossible that it should abide forever free from change, and yet, as far as may be, its movement is uniform, invariable, and in one place. Thus it is that it has been endowed with a rotation in reverse —the least possible variation of its proper motion. To revolve ever by one's own power belongs to none but him who leads all things that move; and even he cannot move the universe now in the one sense, now in the other—for this would flout eternal decrees. For all these reasons there are many doctrines we cannot affirm concerning this universe. We must not say that it moves itself perpetually. We may not say that it is a god who turns it in its entirety throughout all time in two opposed alternating revolutions. We may not say that a pair of divinities who are at cross purposes the one with the other make it revolve. We must therefore affirm the doctrine stated above, which is the one remaining possibility. In the one era it is assisted on its way by the divine cause, receiving a renewal of life from its creator, an immortality of his contriving. In the other era, when it has been released, it moves by its innate force and it has stored up so much momentum at the time of its release that it can revolve in the reverse sense for thousands of revolutions, because its size is so great, its balance so perfect, and the pivot on which it turns so very small.

Y.S. Your whole account seems to me very consistent and very probable.

Str. Let us think about this together. Let us study this event which, we alleged, underlies all these miraculous stories in the light of what we have just said. It is this.

Y.S. What is it?

Str. The fact that the revolution of the heaven is sometimes in its present sense, sometimes in the reverse sense.

Y.S. How would you state its significance?

Str. This change of motion we must regard as the most im-
c portant and the most complete of all "turnings back"[7] occurring in the celestial orbits.

Y.S. It would seem so.

Str. We must believe, then, that at the time such changes take place in the universe we human beings living within it have to undergo the most drastic changes also.

Y.S. That is to be expected.

Str. Do we not know from experience that when great changes of many kinds come upon them at once, all living beings can hardly stand the strain?

Y.S. We do indeed.

Str. So it must needs be that there is widespread destruction of living creatures and especially that only a small remnant of
d the human race survives. Many strange new experiences befall this remnant, but there is one of deeper import than all. It goes hand in hand with the reversal of the motion of the universe, at the moment when the revolution counter to the one now prevalent begins to operate.

Y.S. What is it?

Str. First of all, every living creature remained still at whatever stage of life it had attained. All mortal beings halted on their way to assuming the looks of old age, and each began to
e grow backwards, as it were, toward youth and ever greater tenderness. The white hairs of the older men began to grow dark again; the cheeks of bearded men grew smooth once more and restored to each the long-lost bloom of his youth. The bodies of the young men lost the signs of manhood and,

[7] τροπή (turning) was used first of the solstices, the turning back of the sun at the two *tropics*. It was then transferred to the analogous turning points in the orbits of the planets. The application of the word τροπή to a cosmic reversal here is a deliberate extension of its astronomical meaning.

growing smaller every day and every night, they returned again to the condition of newborn children, becoming like them in mind as well as in body. Next they withered away completely and were wiped out altogether. Moreover the bodies of those who died by violence in that time of crisis exhibited these same changes—and did so with such rapidity that their disappearance took place within a few days. 271

Y.S. But how did living creatures come into being in that era, Sir? How did they produce their offspring?

Str. Clearly, Socrates, it was not of the order of nature in that era to beget children by intercourse. Our legends tell us that once upon a time there was an earthborn race. Now it was this race which at that moment of crisis began to return to life out of the earth. The memory of it has lived on, for it was handed down to us by the earliest of our forebears. These lived in the period directly following the end of the former era of cosmic rotation and came into being at the beginning b of the present one. These ancestors of ours passed on to us these stories of the earthborn which so many wrongly disbelieve nowadays. For I think that we must consider the sequel. It is only to be expected that along with the reversal of the old men's course of life and their return to childhood, a new race of men should arise too—a new race formed from men dead and long laid in earth but now formed in her womb anew and thence returning to life once more. Such resurrection of the dead was in keeping with the cosmic change, all creation being now turned in the reverse direction. This race was (as it needs must be) "born from the earth," save for some few whom a god translated to another destiny; hence comes c the name and hence the legend.

Y.S. Yes, this is fully in keeping with what went before; but tell me about the life of man in the reign of Kronos of which you speak. Did this life obtain in the former world-era or in this one? For clearly a change of direction of sun and stars occurs at both points in history at which the universe changes its sense of rotation.

Str. You have followed the story closely. As for your inquiry d concerning the age when all things come without man's labor, the answer is that this also most certainly belongs to the former cycle, not to the present one. In that era, the god was supreme governor in charge of the actual rotation of the universe as a whole, but divine also and in like manner was the government of its several regions; for these were all portioned out to be provinces under the rule of gods. Over every herd of living creatures throughout all their kinds was set a divine daemon to be its shepherd. Each of them was in every way sufficient for e his flock, so that savagery was nowhere to be found nor preying of creature on creature, nor did war rage nor any strife whatsoever. There were numberless consequences of this divine ordering of the world, but we must leave them all aside save those concerning man, for we must go on to explain the tradition that man's life was spontaneous. A god was their shepherd and had charge of them even as men now have charge of the other creatures inferior to them—for men are closer to the divine than they. When this god was shepherd there were no political constitutions and no personal posses- 272 sion of wives and children. For all men rose up anew into life out of the earth, having no memory of the past. Instead they had fruits without stint from trees and bushes; these needed no cultivation but sprang up spontaneously out of the ground without man's toil. For the most part they disported themselves in the open, needing neither clothing nor couch, for the seasons were blended evenly so as to work them no hurt, and the grass which sprang up out of the earth in abundance made b a soft bed for them. This is the story, Socrates, of the life of men under the government of Kronos. Our present life—said to be under the government of Zeus—you are alive to experience for yourself. But which of these two makes for greater happiness, do you think? Can you give a verdict? And will you do so?

Y.S. No, I cannot decide.

Str. Do you want me to make a tentative decision for you?

Y.S. Yes, please do.

Str. The crucial question is—did the nurslings of Kronos

make a right use of their time? They had abundance of leisure and the ability to converse with the animals as well as with one another. Did they use all these advantages for philosophical c ends? As they associated with one another and with the animals, did they seek to learn from each several tribe of creatures whether its special faculties enabled it to apprehend some distinctive truth not available to the rest which it could bring as its contribution to swell the common treasure store of wisdom? If they really did all this, it is easy to decide that the happiness of the men of that era was a thousandfold greater than ours. But if, when they had taken their fill of eating and of drinking, the discussions they had with each other and with the animals were of the kind that the surviving stories make them out to have been, then, according to my judgment at any rate, it is equally clear what our verdict d must be. But be that as it may, let us leave this question aside till we find someone who can inform us accurately whether or not their hearts were set on gaining knowledge and on engaging in discussion. But we must state the reason why we brought this myth to life, so that we may then be free to proceed to the rest of the story.

For when this whole order of things had come to its destined end, there must needs be universal change once more. For the earthborn race had by now become quite exhausted e—each soul had run through its appointed number of births and had returned as seed to the earth as many times as had been ordained for it. And now the pilot of the universe let go the handle of its rudder, as it were, and retired to his observation tower. Then destiny and its own inborn urge reversed the revolution of the world again. Then the gods of the provinces, who ruled jointly with the greatest god, knew at once what was happening and relinquished the control over their regions. With a jerk the universe changed its rotation, 273 driven by an impulse in which beginning and end reversed their positions. This shock created a great tremor in the universe which caused a new destruction of living creatures of all kinds. Then, after the interval needed for its recovery,

it gained relief at last from its clamors and confusion, and, attaining quiet after the tremors, it returned to its ordered course and continued in it, having control and government of
b itself and of all within it and remembering, so far as it was able, the instruction it had received from its maker and father. At first it fulfilled his instructions more clearly, but as time went on, more carelessly. The bodily element in its constitution was responsible for its failure. This bodily factor belonged to it in its most primeval condition; for before it came into its present order as a universe it was an utter chaos of disorder. It is from him who composed it that it has received all the virtues it possesses, while from its primal chaotic condition all
c the wrongs and troubles that are in heaven arise in it, and these it engenders in turn in the living creatures. When it is guided by the pilot, it produces much good and but little evil in the creatures it raises and sustains. When it must travel on without him, things go well enough in the years immediately after he abandons control, but as time goes on and forgetfulness sets in, the ancient condition of discord also begins to
d assert its sway. At last, as this cosmic era draws to its close, this disorder comes to a head. The few good things it produces it corrupts with so gross a taint of evil that it hovers on the very brink of destruction, both of itself and of the creatures in it.

Therefore, at that very moment, the god looks upon it again, he who first set it in order. Beholding it in its troubles, and anxious for it lest, racked by storms and confusion, it sink and be dissolved again in the bottomless abyss of unlikeness,
e he takes control of the helm once more. Its former sickness he heals; what was disrupted in its former revolution under its own impulse he brings back into the way of regularity; and so, ordering and correcting it, he achieves for it its agelessness and immortality.

This is the full tale told, but to meet our need—the delineation of the king—it is enough if we take up the earlier part of our tale. When the universe turned on its way toward the present order of generation, the course of man's life stood still once more and began to manifest changes in the opposite sense to those which had accompanied the other cosmic crisis. Creatures which were near disappearance because of their smallness began to grow again; those who were just born from the earth now grew snowy-haired and died and returned to the earth again. Following and imitating the change in the universe, all other things had to change, and, in particular, a new law governing conception, birth, and nurture was made binding on all the creatures, for they must imitate its ways. For it was no longer possible for creatures to be brought to birth in the earth by the formative action of external agents. It has now been ordained that the universe must take sole responsibility and control of its course. And so, by a like ruling, the same impulse bade its constituent elements achieve by their own power, so far as they might, conception, procreation, and rearing of young. 274

We have now come to the point which the whole of this story of ours has been seeking to reach. It would take long to tell of all the changes that befell the various creatures and show whence these arose and how they were effected, but man's story is shorter and more relevant for us now. Bereft of the guardian care of the daemon who had owned and tended us, we had become weak and defenseless human beings, and we began to be ravaged by wild beasts—for the many ill-natured beasts had by now turned savage. Men lacked all tools and all crafts in the early years, for their food, which had grown spontaneously, now failed and they did not yet know how to win it for themselves: in the absence of necessity they had never yet been made to learn this. For all these reasons they were in direst straits. It was to meet this need that the gifts of the gods famous in ancient story were given, along with such teaching and education as was indispensable. Fire was the gift of Prometheus, the crafts of Hephaestus and his partner in craftsmanship,[8] and seeds and plants were given b c d

[8] Hephaestus' partner in craftsmanship is Athena. Their common temple in Athens is referred to in *Protagoras*, 321e, under the figure of their common workshop in Olympus whence Prometheus stole the art of working with fire and brought it to men. The "other gods" who revealed the

by other gods. From these gifts everything has come which has furnished human life since the divine guardianship of men ceased (in the way our story has just described) and men had to manage their lives and fend for themselves in the same way as the whole universe was forced to do. Thus imitating the universe and following it through all time, we live and grow at one time in this way and at another time in that.

e Here let our story come to its end, but now we must use it to discern the extent of the mistake we made in our earlier argument in our delineation of the king or statesman.

4. The Revised Definition (274e-277a)

Y.S. How did we go wrong then? Do you think that we are seriously off the track?

Str. One mistake was not so serious, but the other was a mistake on the grand scale; it is graver and more far-reaching than I thought it was.[9]

Y.S. In what way?

Str. We were asked to define the king and statesman of this present cycle and generation, but in fact we took from the

275 contrary cosmic era the shepherd of the human flock as it then was, and described him as the statesman. He is a god, not a mortal. We went far astray in that. Furthermore, we showed him as ruler of all the life of the state but did not specify the manner of his rule. Here too what was said was true, but it cannot be regarded as the whole truth or as a clear and sufficient description. We have gone wrong in this also, though not as badly as on the other issue.

Y.S. True.

---

seeds and plants necessary to men's life were Demeter, Persephone, and Triptolemus. All were worshiped at Eleusis.

[9] The greater mistake was to speak of *nurture* of herds (possible only to shepherds and their like) as distinct from concern for herds (possible also to statesmen) and so to confuse statesmen of today with the "shepherds" under Kronos. The lesser was a failure to distinguish voluntarily accepted tendance from enforced tendance. Later, at 292c, this distinction is challenged.

Str. Obviously, then, we must try to define the way in which the statesman controls the state. We can be reasonably confident that in doing this we shall achieve the complete definition of the statesman.

Y.S. Very good.

Str. But our aim when we introduced the story was to show b two things at once concerning the "nurture of the herd." We were anxious to show the host of rivals with whose claims to be "nurturers of the herd" the statesman whom we seek has to compete; but we were still more anxious to follow out our analogy and to see the statesman himself in a clearer light as being alone entitled to be called "shepherd of the people," caring for humankind in the way shepherds tend their sheep and cowherds their cattle.

Y.S. True.

Str. It appears to me now, Socrates, that the divine shepherd is so exalted a figure that no king can be said to attain to his c eminence. Those who rule these states of ours in this present era are much more like their subjects in nature, and far closer to them in training and in nurture than ever a shepherd could be to his flock.

Y.S. Yes, that is certainly so.

Str. But whether they are human or superhuman creatures, we are still as committed as we were—neither more so nor less —to the task of seeking to reveal their true nature.

Y.S. Of course.

Str. We must go back again for reconsideration of one of our divisions. We said that there is a "predirective" art concerned with living creatures, and with these collectively rather than as individuals. Without further division, we described this as "the science of the *rearing* of herds." You recall this, d do you not?

Y.S. Yes, I do.

Str. It was about at this point that we went astray. We did not catch the statesman at all in this definition or name him properly. He eluded us without our knowing it while we were intent upon the process of naming.

Y.S. How did he do it?

Str. All other herdsmen are charged with the bodily nurture of their herds. This characteristic is absent in the statesman and yet we called him a herdsman. We should have used a
e wider name, covering all guardians, whether nurturers or not.

Y.S. You are right if there is in fact such a name.

Str. Surely "concern" is available as such a class name; it implies no specific limitation to bodily nurture or to any other specific activity. If we had named the art "concern for herds," "attention to herds," or "charge of herds" (all of them terms which cover all species) we could have included the statesman with the rest; for the run of the argument was indicating to us that we ought to do this.

276 *Y.S.* True, but how would the subsequent division have proceeded?

Str. On the same lines as before. We divided "nurture of herds" into nurture of land animals, wingless, non-interbreeding, and hornless. We could have divided "concern for herds" in the same way and our definition would then have included both the kingship under Kronos and that of our present era.

Y.S. That seems clear, but I still want to know what follows.

Str. It is clear that if we had used this correct term, "concern for herds," we should not have had to face the unreason-
b able objection that some make, that ruling is in *no* sense an art of tendance, as well as the other reasonable objection we met that there is no human art of nurture worthy of the name and that, if there were, there would be many with a prior and greater claim to its exercise than any king.

Y.S. True.

Str. But if it is a question of concern for the whole human community, what art has a better or prior claim than the royal art to fulfill this function? What other art can claim to
c be the art of bearing sovereign rule over all men?

Y.S. None can.

Str. Yes, Socrates, but do we realize that we fell into another considerable error at the very end of our definition?

Y.S. What was that?

Str. However clearly we had determined in our minds that there exists an art of nurture of two-footed herds, we were not entitled without further examination to name this art kingship or statesmanship, thereby implying that a full definition of it had been obtained.

Y.S. What should we have done then?

Str. First of all, as we have just been saying, the name has to be modified from "nurture" to "concern." Secondly, this "concern" must be subdivided, for several further divisions are possible. d

Y.S. Which are they?

Str. By one division we should have set apart the divine shepherd and the human tender of men.

Y.S. True.

Str. By another division we should have divided into two the art assigned to this human tender of men.

Y.S. By what division?

Str. By distinguishing enforced tendance from tendance voluntarily accepted.

Y.S. Surely.

Str. I think we really went wrong at this point in our earlier definitions: we made a confusion—a needlessly stupid one—of putting the king and the tyrant into the same class, and these are entirely different people, differing in the manner of their rule. e

Y.S. Yes, they are.

Str. Then let us be right this time, and, as I said, let us divide the art of concern for men into two—enforced tendance and tendance accepted voluntarily.

Y.S. Certainly.

Str. Tendance of human herds by enforced control is the tyrant's art; tendance freely accepted by herds of free bipeds we call statesmanship. Shall we now declare that he who possesses this latter art and practices this tendance is the true king and the true statesman?

Y.S. Yes, and I should think, Sir, that at this point we have really completed our definition of the statesman. 277

5. *The Nature of Example* (277a-279a)

Str. That would be excellent, Socrates; but it is not enough for you to think so: I must think so too. Now as a matter of fact I think that the likeness of the king has not been perfectly drawn yet. Sculptors sometimes rush at their work in ill-timed enthusiasm and then have to make more important additions
b than necessary in elaborating the details so that it slows down their progress. Something like this happened earlier in our discussion, when we wanted to make it immediately clear where we were mistaken and to give a really impressive demonstration of the point. On the assumption that where a king was concerned only large-scale illustrations could be suitable, we reared our massive myth and then had to use more myth-material than the occasion warranted; thus our demonstration became too long and we did not give the myth a complete form after all. Our definition, too, seems to me like a portrait
c which is as yet an outline sketch and does not represent the original clearly because it has still to be painted in colors properly mixed with one another. Remember, however, that a definition couched in words is a better description of a living creature than a drawing or any model of it can be—a better description, I mean, for those capable of following such a definition; for those who cannot do so the model or visible illustration is appropriate enough.

Y.S. Yes, that is true; but please make clear where you still find our description of the statesman inadequate.

d *Str.* It is difficult, my dear Socrates, to demonstrate sufficiently anything of real importance without the use of examples. Every one of us is like a man who sees things in a dream and thinks that he knows them perfectly and then wakes up, as it were, to find that he knows nothing.

Y.S. What do you mean by this?

Str. I have made a real fool of myself by choosing this

moment to discuss our strange human plight where the winning of knowledge is concerned.

Y.S. What do you mean?

Str. Example, my good friend, has been found to require an example.

Y.S. What is this? Say on and do not hesitate for my sake. e

Str. I will—in fact, I must, since you are so ready to follow. When young children have only just learned their letters—

Y.S. Yes? 278

Str. —we know that they distinguish particular letters only adequately in the shortest and simplest syllables; in these, however, they can tell you correctly what each of them is.

Y.S. Yes?

Str. But if they see the same letters combined into other syllables, they fall into doubt once more, and judge and identify them incorrectly.

Y.S. True.

Str. What then is the easiest and best method of leading them to the knowledge they have not yet reached? I think I know it.

Y.S. What is it?

Str. Take them to the syllables in which they have identified the letters correctly, then set them in front of the syllables they cannot yet decipher; then place known syllables and unknown syllables side by side and point out to them the similar b nature of the letters occurring in both. In the end by this method when the rightly identified letters have been shown to them and set alongside all the unknown letters—and by being shown thus the known letters have been used as *examples*—the teacher will achieve his aim, which is to have each letter rightly recognized and named in every syllable; for then the pupil will have identified each letter with itself and distin- c guished it from all the others.

Y.S. Certainly.

Str. Have we not gathered enough information now to show how the method of example proceeds? It operates, does it not, when two identical elements that are found in widely separated areas are correctly believed to be identical, and are brought together so that one true judgment about each of them will result, namely, that they both belong together.

Y.S. That appears to be how it works.

Str. Would we be surprised, then, to find our own mind re-

d acting in the same way to the letters with which the universe is spelled out?[10] Truth sometimes guides the mind to a comprehension of every member of some groups of things and yet the same mind a moment later is hopelessly adrift in its attempt to cope with the members that make up another group. Somehow or other it makes a right judgment of a particular combination of elements, but when it sees the same elements transferred to the long and very difficult syllables of actual facts it fails to recognize again the very elements it discerned a moment before.

Y.S. One cannot wonder at it.

Str. It is impossible, is it not, to achieve real understanding

e in an approach to any part of truth, however small, if one begins from a false opinion?

Y.S. I should say that it is quite impossible.

Str. Well, then, if this is the true state of the case, you and I could claim to be sound in our former method and in what we plan to do now. We have tried to discover the nature of example in general by studying a small and particular example of it. What we intend to do now is to discover scientifically by means of the method of example the nature of "tendance" as applied to the state; and we intend to do it by taking from lesser realms the quality identical with the kingly quality and to use its lesser manifestation there in order to discern its supreme manifestation in him. Then we shall no longer be dreaming but awake.

Y.S. We will hope so.

279 *Str.* So we must take up once again an earlier stage of our discussion; for seeing that there prove to be any number of

[10] The Greek στοιχεῖον (Latin *elementum*) means "letter" and "element" at once.

competitors to dispute with the kingly class the duties of the tendance of states, we must surely set aside all competitors and leave only the king in possession. It was to help us to this end that we decided that we needed to employ an example.

Y.S. True.

6. *The Definition of Weaving* (279a-283b)

Str. Well, then, what example is there on a really small scale which we can take and set beside statesmanship, and which, because it constitutes an activity similar to statesmanship, can be of real help to us in finding what we are looking for? By heaven, Socrates, I believe I know one. Do you agree that, if b there is no other example ready to hand, it would be quite in order for us to select the art of weaving for the purpose? Moreover, if you agree, we will not take the whole of weaving; for I think that a part of it, the art of weaving woolens, will prove adequate for us. I suspect that just this section of the weaver's art, if it were chosen as our example, would give the evidence we require concerning the statesman.

Y.S. Certainly.

Str. Why should we not divide weaving now just as we divided the other classes of things, dividing it into its true parts? We must run through each stage as briefly and quickly as we c can so as to come back to what is relevant to our present discussion.

Y.S. What do you mean?

Str. I can best explain by making the actual division for you.

Y.S. Excellent!

Str. All we make and all we get has one of two aims: the aim of doing something, or the aim of preventing something being done. Preventives may be divided into (*a*) antidotes (divine or human) and (*b*) protections; protections into (*a*) war- d like armaments or defense works and (*b*) other means of fending off; nonmilitary means of fending off into (*a*) screens and (*b*) protections from storm and heat; protections from storm

and heat into (*a*) housing and (*b*) coverings for the person; coverings for the person into (*a*) blankets spread below and (*b*) garments spread around. Garments that we put around us are of one piece or compounded of several. Those compounded of several are either stitched or combined by a method other
e than stitching; of the unstitched some are made of vegetable fibers, others are made of hair; of those made of hair, some are felted by water and earth, others are combined by their inherent substance. To these manufactured means of warding off which are coverings of the person and compacted in their own substance we give the name "clothes." The art specifically concerned with producing clothes we will describe from the name of its product as the "clothes-working" art, just as we
280 called the art of controlling a state statesmanship. We may also say that the art of weaving—or at any rate that very large section of it concerned with the production of clothes—is distinct in nothing but name from this "art of clothes-working," just as in the other case we regarded the arts of kingship and statesmanship as synonymous.

Y.S. Quite right.

Str. Let us observe now that it might be supposed that the
b definition of the art of weaving clothes, as drawn up in these terms, had been sufficient. But if one supposed this, one would have failed to see that the art has not yet been distinguished from arts exercising a function closely similar to it, and that in spite of this many other arts which are akin to it have been severed from it.

Y.S. What are these kindred arts of which you are thinking?

Str. Evidently you are not following what has been said. We must go back then and begin from the other end; for if you really can apprehend affinities between arts you will find that some kindred arts are detached from weaving in our recent division. For instance, in the division of what is put under from what is put around we divided off the art of blanket-making from the art of clothes-making.

Y.S. Yes, I see.

c *Str.* Furthermore, we disjoined from weaving all fabrication of flax, of Spanish broom, and of all the natural products we termed vegetable fibers. We also disjoined from it felting and the art of fashioning by piercing and sewing—the art of which the shoemaker is the chief practitioner.

Y.S. We did.

Str. Then in dividing the art of making garments of one piece we excluded the art of the skinner. Among arts of protective housing we excluded the art of stemming inroads of water along with housebuilding, carpentry, and similar arts. We also excluded all the arts of fencing off, but these include d the arts of preventing theft and other violence, arts connected with making lids and door fastenings normally assigned as sections of the arts of joinery. We also cut off the whole art of armor-making, which is an extensive and extremely various section of the art of producing defenses. Finally we separated off, right at the beginning of our definition, the magician's art and that of making antidotes. The remainder when all these e had been excluded was, we might fairly suppose, the art we had been seeking—the art concerned with producing works of woolen protection designed to ward off violences of climate, called by the name "weaving." [11]

Y.S. Yes, that seems to be accurate.

Str. But we have not yet achieved a complete description of the matter under discussion, my young friend. For it is evident that the man responsible for the first stage in the production of clothes does just the opposite of weaving. 281

Y.S. How do you mean?

Str. The process of weaving is, I take it, a form of plaiting together?

[11] It would be unwise to take Plato seriously about every detail in this paragraph: even the lexicographer Pollux, commenting on words that occur only here in extant literature, expressed the doubt whether Plato was serious—he had "wrenched the words rather violently" (*Onomasticon*, VII, 208-10). The general intention of the passage is to find in *every* stage of the previous division some art with a closely similar activity to "clothes-working" which has been put on the left-hand side of the division and so "separated off" from clothes-making in spite of its being obviously "akin" to it.

Y.S. Yes.

Str. But the art I spoke of is an art of dissociating strands from a mass of material in which they are found close and matted.

Y.S. What is that?

Str. The work done by the art of carding. Dare we call carding weaving, or speak of the carder as a weaver?

Y.S. Certainly not.

Str. Now consider the art which produces warp and woof. If one calls that art "weaving" it sounds odd, but it is more b than that—it is false in fact.

Y.S. Of course.

Str. Furthermore, consider the art of the fuller in all its forms, and that of darning. Are we going to deny that these are, in a sense, arts of tendance or care of clothes? But if we admit that they are such, does it follow that we shall call them all arts of weaving?

Y.S. By no means.

Str. And yet the claim to preside over the care and the production of clothes is a claim which all of these arts dispute with the weaver's art. They are ready to concede to weaving the largest part of the whole province of clothes-working, but at the same time they demand the assignment of no small part of it to themselves.

c *Y.S.* That is very true.

Str. Then in addition to these arts we have to consider the arts which produce the instruments by which the weaving process is carried out. We must suppose that all have their claim to be at least contributory to the making of every piece of fabric.

Y.S. That is so.

Str. Do we still suppose that weaving (or rather our selected portion of it) will have been adequately defined if we declare it to be "the highest and most dignified of all the arts con- d cerned with woolen clothing"? Would not this definition, though true as far as it goes, lack clearness and finality until we have dissociated all these other arts from weaving?

Y.S. It would.

Str. Then our next duty is to make this separation, so that our definition may proceed by the right stages.

Y.S. Yes.

Str. To begin with, let us observe that two groups of arts are involved in everything we do.

Y.S. What are they?

Str. One class contributory to the production, the other actually producing.

Y.S. In what way?

Str. I mean by "contributory" arts those which do not fashion the product itself but prepare the tools for the arts which actually produce it—they are arts without whose previous assistance the specific task of the productive arts could never be performed. The arts which fashion the product itself are the "productive" arts. e

Y.S. That is at any rate a reasonable distinction.

Str. Then may we take the further step of distinguishing arts which manufacture spindles, shuttles, and all the other instruments of clothes manufacture as "contributory arts" from the directly "productive" arts which actually treat and produce the clothes?

Y.S. We certainly may.

Str. Among these "productive" arts those of washing, darning, and general servicing of clothes—the relevant section of the very extensive art of adornment—may fairly be grouped together and we may call the whole group "the art of the fuller." 282

Y.S. Very well.

Str. Carding and spinning and all the other special processes involved in the manufacture of woolen garments together form part of the art of wool-working? This time we have an art with a name familiar to everyone.

Y.S. Of course.

Str. Wool-working has two principal sections: each of them is comprised of arts which are parts of a pair of arts. b

Y.S. What do you mean?

Str. Carding, half the operation of the shuttle, and all the processes which pull strands of close material apart—let us class these together as one art and this art is manifestly part of wool-working. But we must remember, too, the pair of arts we found to be of universal scope, the art of combining and that of separating.

Y.S. Yes.

Str. Well, carding and the other arts just mentioned come c under separation. Thus it is *separation* of the raw wool and *separation* of the strands of warp (the former being done by hand, the latter by the shuttle) which have been given their respective names which we used a moment ago.

Y.S. Very true.

Str. Now let us consider in turn the art of combination and look for the part of it which coincides with part of the art of wool-working. We must now omit all sections of wool-working which come under separation. Then we shall have divided wool-working by distinguishing the part which combines and the part which separates.

Y.S. Let us assume this division.

Str. Then, Socrates, you will find that we have to subdivide d the part of wool-working which combines, if we are to run our quarry to earth by finding the art of weaving which we made our objective.

Y.S. Yes, that we must do.

Str. We must. To name the divisions, let us call one section of the art "twisting" and the other "plaiting."

Y.S. Do I understand you? I take you to mean by "twisting" the art concerned with producing the threads of warp.

Str. Yes, but not of the warp only—of the woof, too. You surely do not imagine that we shall find it produced by some process other than twisting?

Y.S. No.

e *Str.* Now divide each of these two arts: for you may well find this division significant.

Y.S. At what point must I divide?

Str. I will tell you. The finished product of the carding

processes, when it has achieved certain recognized dimensions, we describe as a "flock" of wool.

Y.S. Yes.

Str. The thread twisted out of this by the spindle to form a firm yarn you will, no doubt, describe as "warp" and the art directing its production as warp-spinning.

Y.S. Yes.

Str. But there are other threads from the flock which are only loosely twisted so as to be soft enough for intertwining with the warp but strong enough to stand up to the dressing process after being intertwined with it. These threads we call "woof" and the art superintending their manufacture woof-spinning. 283

Y.S. Quite so.

Str. Well, then, the section of the art of weaving which we selected is now clearly defined for all to see. When the section of the art of combination which is also a section of the art of wool-working produces a fabric by the due intertwining of warp and woof, we call the finished fabric a woolen garment and the art superintending its production the art of weaving.

Y.S. That is perfectly correct.

Str. Good. But why did we not distinguish weaving straight away as the art of intertwining warp and woof? Why did we set about it in this roundabout fashion, defining so pointlessly a host of arts we met on the way? b

Y.S. Oh no, Sir! So far as I can see, there was nothing pointless in the whole course of our argument.

7. *Excess and Deficiency* (283b-287b)

Str. I am not surprised that you think so now, but some day you may think differently, my dear fellow. I want to administer a prophylactic against this malady of doubt, should it one day come upon you, as indeed it well may: there would be nothing surprising in its doing so! Listen, then, to an argument applicable to all troublesome questions of this kind. c

Y.S. Tell me.

Str. First let us examine excess and deficiency in general. In this way we shall obtain a standard of length applicable to what is said on any occasion in this kind of discussion—a standard by which we can accord praise to what is said or censure it as excessive or as deficient.

Y.S. Let us make the examination then.

Str. We can only discuss the matter effectively by considering these qualities in their real nature.

Y.S. Which qualities?

Str. Length and brevity, and excess and defect in general. d We are agreed, I presume, that the art of measurement is involved in all these.

Y.S. Yes.

Str. Let us divide it into two then. We must do so to get to the conclusion we are eager to reach.

Y.S. Please tell us where the division comes.

Str. I will. We divide the art of measurement into a section concerned with the relative greatness or smallness of objects and another section concerned with their size in relation to the fixed norm to which they must approximate if they are to exist at all.

Y.S. What do you mean?

Str. Do you not agree that in the nature of things "the greater" can be so called only in relation to the less and to nothing else; and, conversely, that "the less" can only be "less" e than a greater? It cannot be "less" than anything else.

Y.S. I quite agree.

Str. On the other hand, will we not also be ready to assert that we do in fact hear words spoken and see acts done which at one time exceed the essentially right measure and at another time are exceeded by it? Is it not just this matter of attaining the due measure which marks off good men from bad?

Y.S. It is evident.

Str. Then we must posit two types and two standards of greatness and smallness. We must not assert as we did just now that the only standard possible is that of relative comparison.

We have just seen how we must amend the statement. The standard of relative comparison will remain, but we must acknowledge a second standard, which is a standard of comparison with the due measure. Do we want to know why this must be admitted?

Y.S. By all means.

Str. If a man refuses to admit the possibility of a "greater" except in relation to a "lesser," he will rule out all possibility of relating it to a due measure, will he not? 284

Y.S. He will.

Str. Are we really prepared for the consequences of this refusal? Are we going to abolish the arts and all their products? In particular, shall we deprive statecraft (which we are trying to define) and weaving (which we have just defined) of their very existence? For it seems clear to me that all such arts guard against exceeding the due measure or falling short of it. Certainly they do not treat such excess or defect as nonexistent—on the contrary, they shun it as a very real peril when it comes to action. In fact, it is precisely by this effort they make to maintain the due measure that they achieve effectiveness and beauty in all that they produce. b

Y.S. That is very true.

Str. But you must admit that if we nullify statecraft, we shall have blocked all means of approach to any subsequent study of the science of kingly rule.

Y.S. Obviously.

Str. Must we not do now what we had to do when discussing the sophist? We felt constrained to admit that "what is 'not x' nevertheless exists," because the only alternative which our argument left us was to allow the sophist to escape definition altogether. In our present discussion, too, we have to admit that excess and deficiency are measurable not only in relative terms but also in respect of attainment of a norm or due measure. For if we cannot agree on this, we are bound to fail if we advance the claim that a man possesses statecraft, or indeed that a man possesses any other of the special forms of knowledge that function in human society. c

Y.S. In that case we must certainly follow the precedent in our present discussion too.

Str. Our present task is greater than the previous one, Socrates, and we can hardly have forgotten what a very long time that took us. However, while discussing these problems, there is one thing to be said at the outset that it is perfectly right and proper to say here.

Y.S. What is this?

d *Str.* That when some day we come to give a full and accurate exposition of this subject, we shall need what we have just enunciated concerning due measure. However, the statement in the form that we have made it and with the demonstration (adequate for present purposes) which we have given of it is a very great help to us, or so it seems to me. For it shows, first, that the arts exist, and second, that excess and deficiency are measurable not only relatively but in terms of the realization of a norm or due measure. Thus, if due measure exists, so do the arts; and conversely, if there are arts, then there is due measure. To deny either is to deny both.

e *Y.S.* So much is fully established, but what follows?

Str. Clearly, we should divide the art of measurement into two on the principle enunciated by dividing it at this point. One section will comprise all arts of measuring number, length, depth, breadth, or velocity of objects by relative standards. The other section comprises arts concerned with due measure, due occasion, due time, due performance, and all such standards as have removed their abode from the extremes and are now settled about the mean.

Y.S. Each of the subdivisions you have named is very extensive, and the one differs vastly from the other.

Str. Does not the statement we have just made turn out to
285 be precisely what many of our erudite friends [12] say from time

[12] The reference is evidently to the Pythagoreans. They are here commended for seeing that the art of measurement is relevant to the whole process of coming into being, but they are censured for failing to distinguish the two kinds of measurement (and thus, presumably, for making statements like "things are numbers") because they do not employ the Platonic dialectic which would make the distinction clear to them.

to time—and say with the air of men uttering a profound truth? We are saying like them that measurement is involved in all that is brought into being. For all activities directed by arts involve measuring in some form or other. But our friends, for all their erudition, have not been trained to study things by dividing them into real classes. As a result, here we find them confusing these two types of measurement, which are in fact so different, just because they believe them to be of like nature. There are other classes of things about which they commit the opposite error: they distinguish them but fail to distinguish according to the real distinctions. Now the following would be the right method. Whenever it is the essential *affinity* between a given group of forms which the philosopher perceives on first inspection, he ought not to forsake his task until he sees clearly as many true differences as exist within the whole complex unity—the differences which exist in reality and constitute the several species. Conversely, when he begins by contemplating all the *unlikenesses* of one kind or another which are to be found in a multitude of things, the true philosopher must not pull a wry face and give up in disgust, until he has gathered together all the forms which are in fact cognate and has penned them safely in their common fold by comprehending them all in their real general class. But let this suffice on these topics and on excess and deficiency in general. Let us, however, be careful to maintain the ground we have won. We have discovered beyond dispute two distinct forms of the art of measurement concerned with excess and deficiency and we must remember what we have declared them to be.

b

c

Y.S. We shall not forget.

Str. So much for that theme. Now let us prepare to entertain another which has to do not only with our present inquiry but with all discussions of this kind as well.

Y.S. What is it?

Str. Suppose someone asked us this question about our class of elementary-school children learning to read.[13] When a child

[13] *Cf.* 277e.

is asked what letters spell a word—it can be any word you please—are we to regard this exercise as undertaken to discover d the correct spelling of the particular word the teacher set or as designed rather to make the child better able to deal with all words he may be asked to spell?

Y.S. Surely the purpose is to teach him to read them all.

Str. How, then, does this principle apply to our present search for the statesman? Why did we set ourselves the problem? Is our chief purpose to find the statesman, or have we the larger aim of becoming better dialecticians, more able to tackle all questions?

Y.S. Here, too, the answer is clear; we aim to be able to solve all problems.

Str. Exactly, for I cannot think that any reasonable person would want to track down the definition of the art of weaving just for its own sake. But there is one thing which, it seems to me, most people have failed to notice. Some of the things that e have true existence and are easy to understand have likenesses in nature which are accessible to the senses, so that when someone asks for an account of any one of them one has no trouble at all—one can simply point to the sensible likeness and dispense with any account in words. But to the highest and most important class of existents there are no correspond- 286 ing visible resemblances, no work of nature clear for all to look upon. In these cases nothing visible can be pointed out to satisfy the inquiring mind: the instructor cannot cause the inquirer to perceive something with one or other of his senses and so make him really satisfied that he understands the thing under discussion. Therefore we must train ourselves to give and to understand a *rational* account of every existent thing. For the existents which have no visible embodiment, the existents which are of highest value and chief importance, are demonstrable only by reason and not by any other means. All our present discussions have the aim of training us to apprehend them. For purposes of practice, however, it is easier in b every case to work on lesser rather than on greater objects.

Y.S. You are quite right.

Str. Let us then recall what led us to this long digression on these matters.

Y.S. What was it?

Str. Was it not mainly due to the impatience we felt and expressed at the longwindedness (as we presumed to call it) of our definition of the art of weaving? We felt alike impatience with the long account of reversal of rotation in the universe and with our inquiry into the sophist when we had to discuss the existence of not-being. We conceived the notion that these discussions had been too lengthy, and we blamed ourselves for this because we feared that they had been irrelevant, too. c Please realize, therefore, that the principles we have just worked out together apply to all discussions of this kind, and that they are intended to prevent any like apprehensions in the future.

Y.S. All right. Please proceed.

Str. I say then that it is your duty and mine to observe the principles we have just laid down whenever we have to praise or blame an argument on the score of its length or its brevity. The length of one discourse is not to be compared simply with the length of another. We said just now that we must never forget the second section of the art of measuring, and it is this d standard we must always apply in judgments like these—the standard of suitability, I mean.

Y.S. Quite so.

Str. Yes, but even suitability is not in every case an adequate criterion. For instance, we shall not look for such length in an argument as is "suitable" for giving pleasure, except as a very incidental consideration. Again, ease and speed in reaching the answer to the problem propounded are most commendable, but our principle requires that this be only a secondary, not a primary reason for commending an argument. What we must value first and foremost, above all else, is the systematic investigation itself, and this consists in ability to divide according to real forms. If, therefore, either a full-length statement of an argument or an unusually brief one e leaves the hearer more able to find real forms, it is this presentation of it which must be diligently carried through; there must be no expression of annoyance at its length or at its brevity. Furthermore, if we find a man who criticizes the length of an argument while a discussion like the present one is in progress and refuses to wait for the proper rounding-off of the process of reasoning, he must not give up so quickly without any ado, with a mere grumble that "these discussions 287 are long-drawn-out"; he must be required to support his grumble with a proof that a briefer statement of the case would have left him and his fellow disputants better dialecticians, more able to demonstrate real truth by reasoned argument. Blame and praise on other grounds, aimed at other merely incidental traits in our discourse, we must simply ignore and act as though we had not heard them at all. Now we may leave this topic, if you agree. Let us go back to the states- b man and apply to him the example of the art of weaving as we have just defined it.

Y.S. Excellent. Let us do as you say.

8. The Final Definition of the Statesman (287b-300e)

(a) Distinguished from Primary Producers (287b-289d)

Str. Well, then, the kingly art has been set apart from most of those occupying the same region—from all, that is to say, which have to do with control of herds. But in the actual community of citizens there are other arts not yet distinguished from statesmanship. They comprise both contributory and directive productive arts, and these must first be distinguished from one another.

Y.S. Very well.

Str. Do you realize that it is hard to divide these arts into c two? I think that the reason will become evident to us as we go on.

Y.S. Let us do so then.

Str. Seeing that we cannot bisect them, let us divide them according to their natural divisions as we would carve a sacrificial victim.[14] For we must in every case divide into the minimum number of divisions that the structure permits.

Y.S. How shall we do it then, in the present instance?

Str. As we did before. All the arts which provide tools for weaving we distinguished as contributory.

Y.S. We did.

Str. We must do the same now as then, but with even greater care. Every art which fashions any object, large or small, which ministers to the needs of a state must be classed as "contributory." For without the things provided by these arts there could be no state and so no art of statesmanship; and yet we can hardly regard it as the function of the kingly art to produce any of these things. d

Y.S. No.

Str. We are attempting a difficult thing when we try to distinguish this class of arts from the others. For anything whatever can be shown with some plausibility to be a tool or means to something or other. However, there is a class of things a state must acquire to which we must give a different name. e

Y.S. In what way different?

Str. In that its function differs from that of instruments. It is not made, as an instrument is, with a view to the production of something but in order to preserve a thing once it has been produced.

Y.S. What kind of thing do you mean?

Str. A class of objects wrought in the greatest variety of shapes and used for holding liquids or solids, for what has been prepared in the fire or without fire. As a general name we term such an object a "container." It is a ubiquitous class of objects and has, I think, nothing whatever to do with the art of the ruler which we are now seeking. 288

Y.S. Nothing at all.

Str. We must now recognize a third class of things to be acquired, also a very large one. Some things belonging to it are on land, others on water; some move from place to place, oth-

[14] I.e., at their natural joints. [Ed.]

ers do not; some are of high honor, others are not so distinguished. All share one name because each is made to support something or serve as a base for something.

Y.S. What common name have they?

Str. "Carriage," I should say—and the production of such things is the work of the carpenter, the potter, or the coppersmith, but not of the statesman.

Y.S. I understand.

b *Str.* What is our fourth class? Must we not distinguish from all these three a further class to which most of the things mentioned in our definition of weaving belong—the whole class of clothing, most armor, all walls, all earth or stonework defenses erected around a city, and many other such things? All are made for defensive protection and so the whole class can best be called "defenses." To provide these is in most cases regarded as the work of the builder or weaver, rather than that of the statesman.

Y.S. Of course.

c *Str.* Might we posit a fifth class including all decorative and graphic arts and every art which produces artistic representations, whether in these visual arts or for the ear in poetry and music? The works of all these arts are designed simply to give pleasure, and all may properly be included under one term.

Y.S. What is that?

Str. We use the expression "diversion," do we not?

Y.S. Yes, what of it?

Str. Then this is the name we can properly apply to the products of this whole group of arts. None of them has a serious purpose; all are performed for pure amusement.

d *Y.S.* I think I understand this too.

Str. Consider now that art which provides the stuffs which are wrought by the arts we have been talking about. This is a most various class of arts. Often such an art is itself working on the products of several yet more primitive arts. Shall we not take this as the sixth kind?

Y.S. Of what are you thinking?

Str. Gold and silver and all mined metals; all the pioneer work done by woodcutting and lopping to provide material for carpentry and wickerwork; the currier's art which removes the skins of animals, the art of stripping bark which has the same function in the plant realm, and all arts kindred to these; the arts of making cork, papyrus, and rope. All these arts produce the main types of raw material for working up simple things into the more complex kinds of objects which we use. Let us call this class of object by the general description "basic material at the stage of its first working when it is still the simple possession of man"; and the production of this is obviously no concern of the kingly science. e

Y.S. True.

Str. We come lastly to the getting of food and of all the substances the parts of which are capable of combining with the parts of the body to promote its health. This we will make a seventh class and call it "nourishment" unless we can find some better name for it. Provision of it is rightly to be assigned to the arts of farming, hunting, gymnastic, medicine, or cooking, rather than to political science. 289

Y.S. Of course.

Str. I think that possessions of practically every kind that we find belonging to men have been enumerated in these seven classes, with the single exception of tame living creatures. Listen while I run through the list. First place in it should really have been taken by "basic material at its first working"; after that come instruments, then vessels, carriages, defenses, diversions, and nourishments. We may neglect any class of merely slight importance which may have escaped us, for it can be made to fit in one or other of these main classes. For example, consider the class consisting of coins, seals, and every other kind of engraved dies.[15] These do not have what it takes to be made into one of the great classes; some have to be subsumed under "ornaments," some under "instruments"; it is a forced classification, but they can be made to harmonize with one or b

[15] The reference would seem to be to engraved gems, like enough to the coins to be naturally classified with them. These are "diversions," the coins are "instruments"—a means of exchange, in fact.

the other of these classes completely. As for tame animals other
c than slaves, all these clearly come under the art of nourishing herds which we have previously analyzed.[16]

Y.S. Yes, they do.

Str. The class that remains, then, is that of slaves and personal servants of all kinds. It is just here that I strongly suspect that those will be discovered who really dispute the fashioning of the web of state with the king in the way that we found spinners, carders and the rest disputing the fashioning of clothes with the weavers. All the others, since they pursue what we have described as "contributory" arts, have been disposed of along with their functions which we have enumerated just now, and thus they have all been severed from any share
d in the kingly art of ruling the state.

Y.S. So at any rate it would seem.

Str. Come then, let us examine the rest and approach them more closely to scrutinize them more effectively.

Y.S. Let us do so.

(b) Distinguished from Slaves, Laborers, and Merchants (289d-290a)

Str. The most extensive class of servants, as seen from our new vantage point, we find to be engaged in pursuits and sunk in a condition of life quite contrary to those we had suspected we might discover.

Y.S. To whom do you refer?

Str. To those who are bought and sold and so become their master's property. No one would think of challenging our de-

[16] It is noteworthy that Plato does not regard the slave as a living tool as Aristotle does in the *Politics* (I, 3, 1253b, 28). He is therefore classed not as an "instrument" but in the rather vague residual class of live possessions, as a kind of "tame living creature." The hint at 309a below is in accord with this. The *Laws* make it quite clear, however, that the slave is a piece of property and suggests that he is not always "tame" (*Laws,* VI, 777). Similarly the sale of a diseased slave is treated legally like the sale of defective wares in *Laws,* XI (915e ff.).

scription of these as slaves or our contention that they cannot possibly claim any share in the kingly art.[17] e

Y.S. That goes without saying.

Str. But what of servants who are personally free? What of those among them who of their own volition place themselves and their services at the disposal of the various craftsmen we have named and effect a systematic distribution of agricultural and manufactured products, maintaining an economic balance between them? Some of these do their work at home in the market place, but others are travelers from city to city, overland and by sea. They exchange money for goods or one currency for another. Our names for them are money-changers, merchants, shipowners, retailers. They cannot be said to dispute the province of the ruler, can they? 290

17 Why does Plato suggest that the statesman will be discovered among "slaves and other subordinates"? Is it simply because all the arts discussed up to now have been subordinate arts providing the material assets which are the *sine qua non* of the life of a community, and now at last we have come to the various personal "services" (as we should call them, though they are still arts for Plato) and the statesman must be somewhere in this main group as distinct from the other? Probably there is a deeper reason grounded on the aristocratic sense of *noblesse oblige* which characterized Plato himself. It shows itself in the *Republic* in the insistence that the philosopher, once illumined by the Good, must return to the Cave. It appears again, more specifically connected with the expressions "slavery" and "menial service" in the *Laws,* VI, 762c. Any man needs to have been a slave before he can be a good master—a slave, that is, to the laws, to the gods, and to honored senior members of his community. The young rural commissioners must be their own (and each other's) "deacons" or batmen, and may only call on the farmers to supply "hands" for public enterprises. The statesman is to be the Prime Minister of the community, but not one "bought" (i.e., by bribery) and so a slave in the bad sense of the term.

It should also be noted that in the *Gorgias* (517b ff.) the average "politician" is regarded as one who *"ministers"* only to the physical requirements of a state, or rather, who panders to its desires: he is there contrasted with the true statesman who knows its real needs. Now, however, the phrase "servant of the community" is given a higher sense. We must not be oblivious to the force and novelty of the change because we are tempted to be cynical about such "ministers" after nearly 2,500 years of experience.

Y.S. I wonder if they might—in the realm of commerce, that is to say.[18]

Str. Certainly not. You can be sure that such men who can be hired for pay, who work for a daily wage and who are always ready to work for any employer, will never be found daring to claim any share in the kingly art.

Y.S. No, of course not.

(c) Distinguished from Clerks, Soothsayers, and Priests (290a-290e)

Str. But there are those who render other kinds of service.

Y.S. What kinds of service? Whom do you mean?

b *Str.* Heralds and clerks (who often develop great facility from long performance of their form of service) and certain other very able minor civil servants who do all manner of administrative work. What shall we call them?

[18] There seems to be an implied criticism of commercial magnates here and perhaps, in particular, of banking interests. There do not seem to have been state loans by *banks* in the fourth century, yet the position reflected in the *Trapeziticus* of Isocrates in the first decade of the century is one in which the bank of Pasion already has considerable power over the son of the dynast of the Bosporos, and the later expansion of "the house of Pasion" implied much indirect control of affairs through private loans to politically important persons. Plato is well aware of the danger of such power wielded behind the scenes and this is shown by his strict refusal in the *Laws* to permit the granting of credit and lending at interest (742b ff.), his provision for strict supervision of a retail trade confined to foreigners, and his insistence on the departure of freedmen and resident aliens after twenty years' sojourn (915a, 920a). (See further T. R. Glover, *From Pericles to Philip,* chap. 10; H. Michell, *The Economics of Ancient Greece* (Cambridge University Press, 1940), pp. 335-51.)

The difference between the "merchant" and the "shipowner" was that the latter owned his ship and sailed in it with his own cargo (and occasionally with spare room for other cargo), while the merchant went as a passenger on another man's ship with his wares. Later the term came to mean rather what we mean by merchant and did not always imply that a man was an "emporos" or passenger; but the "merchant" and the "retailer" are probably intended to be distinguished in this way in the present passage. On the distinctions involved see J. Hasebroek, *Trade and Politics in Ancient Greece* (London: G. Bell & Sons, 1933), pp. 1-6.

Y.S. What you just called them—civil servants, but not rulers exercising an independent authority in the state.

Str. I was not cheated by a mere dream, I think, when I said that it was here that the king's serious challengers in the art of rule would reveal themselves. But how strange to have to look for them in a servant class! c

Y.S. Very strange.

Str. Now let us tackle those we have not yet put under examination. First come the soothsayers, practicing their particular form of expert ministration, for they are sometimes regarded as interpreters of the gods to men.[19]

Y.S. Yes.

Str. Next come the priestly tribe. According to the orthodox view, they understand how to offer our gifts to the gods in sacrifices in a manner pleasing to them, and they know, too, d the right forms of prayers for petitioning the gods to bestow blessings on us. Both of these expert activities are parts of the art of ministration,[20] are they not?

[19] The soothsayers (*manteis*) were distinctly more powerful than the minor civil servants. They had a very considerable influence on political events. The implication here is that Plato considered the soothsayers of his own time to be unauthorized political influences. This is explicit at *Laws,* X, 908d. Disbelievers in his official theology can be moral or immoral. Of the immoral we are told: "This is the type that furnishes our swarms of diviners and fanatics for all kinds of imposture; on occasion it also produces dictators, demagogues, generals, contrivers of private Mysteries and the arts and tricks of the so-called 'Sophist' " (trans. A. E. Taylor). However, at *Laws,* VIII, 828b, we are told that the state calendar of religious rites will be controlled, under Delphi's guidance, by a committee of exegetes (chosen by Apollo), priests, priestesses, *and soothsayers* together with the Guardians of the Laws; so the soothsayer will exist in the community envisaged in the *Laws.*

[20] Priests differed essentially from soothsayers in that they were attached to a particular shrine with particular duties. (Of course there were oracular shrines of which Delphi, with its priestess, was most important, but though such a shrine was a *manteion,* its priest would not be a *mantis.*) There were a multitude of shrines with varying rites, each attended by at least one priest. The same deity was worshiped by a different rite or use at different shrines, and there was no co-ordination of such worship. Moreover, a priest might have to perform all the duties

Y.S. Well, it would seem that they are.

Str. In that case I think that we are coming at last upon the tracks of our quarry, so to speak. For the priest and the soothsayer have great social standing and a keen sense of their own importance. They win veneration and respect because of the high tasks they undertake. This is shown in the fact that in Egypt none can be king unless he belongs to the priestly caste, e and if a man of some other caste succeeds in forcing his way to the throne, he must then be made a priest by special ordination.[21] In many of the Greek cities also one finds that the duty of making the chief sacrifice on the state's behalf is laid upon the chief officers of state. You have a very striking example of it here in Athens, for I am led to understand that the

---

of a shrine from sweeping the floor to sacrificing. His duties might be full-time or limited to festival seasons; he might serve for a short period or be appointed for life. The social importance and influence of the priesthood (or rather of the priests) therefore varied very much, but all temple rituals were considered to function on the basic principle Plato here enumerates—the deity received veneration in a prescribed form and heard properly presented petitions, the votary received blessings from the god, and contact between them was established by the service of the priest as the official mediator. There were certain families in which priesthoods of great public importance were hereditary, and it is probably to some of these families that Plato alludes in what follows.

[21] It is not clear to what particular Egyptian custom Plato refers, and his statement does not seem to be grounded in fact. The king was by virtue of his office also a priest, but he could hardly be said to belong to the priestly caste and there seems no evidence for special ordination of members of other "castes" who seized the throne. Who would such usurpers be? Hardly the Persian Achaemenids, for though they took on kingly titles and duties in Egypt (see H. R. Hall, *Cambridge Ancient History,* III, 311) there is no evidence of their becoming priests. Could Plato have known anything of the Shepherd Kings (the Hyksos) who were Semitic invaders who seized Memphis? Plato mentions the Saitic nome at *Timaeus,* 21e, and the scholiast refers to Saites, the first "Shepherd" King, after whom it was named; but this, of course, is no evidence that Plato himself knew the reason for its name. The tradition that Plato himself visited Egypt is uncertain; it is rather more likely that Eudoxus, who was at the Academy at this time, did so. He may be the origin of the statement in this passage.

most solemn ancestral sacrifices of this country are the responsibility of the archon whom the lot designates as King-Archon.[22]

Y.S. That is so.

(d) Distinguished from Politicians (291a-292a)

Str. Very well, we must study these kings chosen by lot and these priests with their ministerial assistants very closely. But we must also look at another group—quite a large mob, in fact, which is coming clearly into view now that all these particular groups have been distinguished. 291

Y.S. And who are these you speak of?

Str. A very queer crowd.

Y.S. What do you mean?

Str. A race of many tribes—or so they seem to be at first sight. Some are like lions, some like centaurs or similar monsters. A great many are like satyrs and weak, versatile beasts b who can quickly assume each other's shapes and abilities. Yes, Socrates, and I think I have now identified these gentlemen.

Y.S. Tell me about them; you seem to look upon a strange sight.

Str. Yes, strange until recognized. I was actually impressed by them myself at first sight. Coming suddenly on this troupe of players acting their part in public life I did not know what c to make of them.

Y.S. What players can these be?

Str. The chief wizards among all the sophists, the chief pundits of the deceiver's art. Such impersonators are hard to distinguish from the real statesmen and kings, yet we must distinguish them and thrust them aside if we are to see clearly what we are seeking.

22 The King-Archon maintained the priestly functions of the original monarchy, but was nevertheless elected by lot; the Stranger seems to wish to note the paradox of this. There is some evidence of magistrates called "kings" elsewhere—at Megara and Samothrace, for example, while in many of the Ionian islands and at Miletus there were "kings" whose duties were purely sacrificial.

Y.S. Well, we must not abandon the search.

Str. No, I agree. Tell me this now.

Y.S. Well?

d *Str.* Is not monarchy one of the possible forms of government as we know it?

Y.S. Yes.

Str. Next to monarchy one would naturally mention the constitution in which the few wield power.

Y.S. Yes.

Str. Then the third type must be the rule of the many—democracy, as it is called.

Y.S. Of course.

Str. These are the three main constitutions, but do not the three in a sense become five by evolving two further types out of themselves? [23]

Y.S. What are these?

e *Str.* If we consider the violence or consent, the poverty or riches, the law-abidingness or disregard of law which they exhibit, we shall find that two of the three forms of government are really twofold and can therefore be divided. Monarchy then yields us two forms, called tyranny and constitutional monarchy respectively.

Y.S. Yes.

Str. Constitutions where the few wield power can always be similarly divided: the subdivisions are aristocracy and oligarchy.

Y.S. Quite so.

Str. In the case of democracy we do not usually alter the name. Democracy is always "democracy" whether the masses

292 control the wealthy by force or by consent and whether or not it abides strictly by the laws.

Y.S. That is true.

Str. What then? Do we imagine that any of these constitu-

[23] The division into three was normal and accepted but the division into five seems to belong to the thought of the Academy. It appears at Diogenes Laertius III, 82, among the "divisions" said on the authority of Aristotle to be Platonic.

tions can be declared a "true" constitution so long as the only criteria for defining it are whether one, few, or many rule; whether it be rich or poor, whether it rule by violence or consent, whether it have or lack a code of laws?

(e) True Statesmanship an Art above All Laws (292a-300e)

Y.S. Why not?

Str. Try to follow what I am going to say and you will be bound to see more clearly. b

Y.S. What line are you going to take?

Str. Shall we abide by our original argument or are we now going against it?

Y.S. Which argument do you mean?

Str. We decided, did we not, that the art of kingly rule is one of the sciences?

Y.S. Yes.

Str. Furthermore, we agreed that it is a particular kind of science. Out of the whole class of sciences we selected the judging class and more particularly the directive class.

Y.S. We did.

Str. We divided the directive into direction of lifeless things and direction of living beings, and by this process of subdivision we arrived by regular stages where we are now, never losing sight of the fact that statesmanship is a form of knowledge but unable as yet to say precisely what form of knowledge it is. c

Y.S. You are quite right.

Str. Do we realize, then, that the real criterion in defining constitutions must not be whether few or many rule, whether rule is by consent or not by consent, or whether the rulers are poor or rich? If we are going to abide by our previous conclusions, the criterion must be the presence or absence of some science.

Y.S. Yes, for we simply must abide by those conclusions. d

Str. Then we are forced to look at the issue in this light. In which, if any, of these constitutions do we find the science of ruling being practiced in the actual government of men? What science is more difficult to learn? But what science is more important to us? We must see it for what it is so as to be able to decide which are the other public figures we must remove from the wise king's company, those personages who claim to be statesmen, who win over the mass of men to believe them to be statesmen, but are in actual fact nothing of the kind.

Y.S. We must indeed, for this was the task set for our discussion.

e *Str.* Do you think that any considerable number of men in a particular city will be capable of acquiring the science of statesmanship?

Y.S. That is quite out of the question.

Str. In a city with a population of a thousand, could a hundred, say, acquire it satisfactorily—or could fifty, perhaps?

Y.S. Statesmanship would be the easiest of the arts if so many could acquire it. We know quite well that there would never be fifty first-class draughts players among a thousand inhabitants—that is, not if they were judged by proper inter-Hellenic standards. How much less can you expect to find fifty kings! For according to our former argument it is only the

293 man possessed of the science of kingship who must be called a king, regardless of whether he is in power or not.

Str. You have very rightly recalled that point. I think it follows that if a true government is to be found at all, it will be found in the possession of one or two, or at most, of a select few.

Y.S. Yes.

Str. On this principle it is the men who possess the art of ruling and these only whom we are to regard as rulers. It makes no difference whether their subjects be willing or unwilling; they may rule with or without a written code of laws, they may be poor or wealthy. It is the same with doctors. We do not assess the medical qualification of a doctor by the de-

b gree of willingness or unwillingness on our part to submit to his knife or cautery or other painful treatment. Doctors are still doctors whether they work according to written rules or without them, and whether they be poor or wealthy. So long as they control our health on a scientific basis, they may purge and reduce us or they may build us up, but they still remain doctors. The one essential condition is that they act for the good of our bodies to make them better instead of worse, and treat men's ailments in every case as healers acting to preserve life. We must insist, I think, that this alone constitutes the true criterion of the science of medicine—and of any other true art of ruling as well. c

Y.S. Quite so.

Str. Then the true constitution par excellence, the only constitution worthy of the name, must be the one in which the rulers are not men making a show of political cleverness but men really possessed of scientific understanding of the art of government. Then we must not take into consideration on any sound principle of judgment whether their rule be by laws or without them, over willing or unwilling subjects, or whether they themselves be rich men or poor men. d

Y.S. No.

Str. They may purge the city for its better health by putting some of the citizens to death or banishing others. They may lessen the citizen body by sending off colonies like bees swarming off from a hive, or they may bring people in from other cities and naturalize them so as to increase the number of citizens. So long as they work on a scientific principle following justice and act to preserve and improve the life of the state so far as may be, we must call theirs the only true constitution according to these standards of judgment. We must go on to say that all the other so-called constitutions are not genuine and have no real existence; they imitate the true constitution. Those which we call law-abiding copy it fairly closely, but the rest are shocking caricatures of it. e

Y.S. Everything you have said, Sir, seems fair enough; but what you say about ruling without laws is a hard thing for us to hear.

Str. You are a little too quick for me, Socrates! I was just going to cross-examine you to see if you really accepted all I 294

have said or felt some objection. I realize, however, from what you say that the point we want to discuss in detail is the question whether a good ruler can govern without laws.

Y.S. Yes, it is.

Str. In one sense it is evident that the art of kingship does include the art of lawmaking. But the best thing of all is not full authority for laws but rather full authority for a man who understands the art of kingship and has wisdom. Do you understand why?

Y.S. No, please tell me why.

Str. Law can never issue an injunction binding on all which really embodies what is best for each; it cannot pre-
b scribe with accuracy what is best and just for each member of the community at any one time. The differences of human personality, the variety of men's activities, and the restless inconstancy of all human affairs make it impossible for any art whatsoever to issue unqualified rules holding good on all questions at all times. I suppose that so far we are agreed.

Y.S. Most emphatically.

Str. But we find practically always that the law tends to
c ignore just this invariable kind of rule. It is like a self-willed, ignorant man who lets no one do anything but what he has ordered and forbids all subsequent questioning of his orders even if the situation has shown some marked improvement on the one for which he originally legislated.

Y.S. Yes, that is just how the law treats us all.

Str. It is impossible, then, for something invariable and unqualified to deal satisfactorily with what is never uniform and constant.

Y.S. I am afraid it is impossible.

Str. But why, then, must laws be enacted, seeing that law is
d not the best form of control? We must find out the reason for that.

Y.S. We must.

Str. You have courses of training here in Athens, have you not, just as they have in other cities—courses in which pupils are trained in a group for athletic contests in running or in other sports?

Y.S. Of course. We have quite a number of them.

Str. Let us call to mind the commands which professional trainers give to the athletes under their regimen in these courses.

Y.S. In what particular?

Str. The view such trainers take is that they cannot do their work in detail and issue special commands adapted to the physical condition of each member of the group. Rather, they think they ought to work in a less refined manner and give a kind of instruction that will be conducive to the general e physical well-being of the majority.

Y.S. Quite so.

Str. That is why we find them giving the same exercises to whole groups of pupils, starting or stopping all of them at the same time in their running, wrestling, or whatever it may be.

Y.S. Yes.

Str. Similarly, we must expect that the legislator who has to preside over herds in matters of right and of mutual contractual obligation will never be able in the laws he prescribes for 295 the whole group to give every individual his due with absolute accuracy.

Y.S. Very probably not.

Str. But we shall find him making the law for the majority of his subjects under average circumstances. Thus he will legislate for all individual citizens, but it will be in a somewhat less refined manner by making a written code of law or by issuing laws that are unwritten but embody ancestral customs.[24]

[24] The "unwritten laws" in this context are of course not (1) some kind of "equity" by which the rigor of the literal application of a written law is mitigated; or (2) some universal law naturally accepted by all mankind. They are, rather, a set of traditions that are no less binding—and probably even more so—than the written statutes of a state, but binding only within the confines of the state and its community. The peculiar thing for us here is that the Greeks envisaged the possibility that such unwritten laws had a beginning in time and could be enacted by a lawgiver.

Y.S. Yes, and quite rightly so.

Str. Of course he is right, Socrates. How could any lawgiver be capable of prescribing every act of a particular individual b and sit at his side all through his life telling him what to do? And if among those who have grasped the true science of kingship there were someone capable of doing that, I think he would hardly put obstacles in his own way by framing written codes of the kind we have been criticizing.

Y.S. That certainly follows, Sir, from what has been said.

Str. I would rather say, my dear friend, that it follows from what is going to be said.

Y.S. And what is that?

Str. Let us put this case to ourselves. A doctor or trainer c plans to travel abroad and expects to be away from his charges for quite a long time. The doctor might well think that his patients would forget any verbal instructions he gave and the trainer might think likewise. In these circumstances each might want to leave written reminders of his orders—do you not think so?

Y.S. Exactly so, Sir.

Str. Well now, suppose our doctor did not stay abroad as long as he had expected and so came back the sooner to his patients. Would he hesitate to substitute different prescriptions for the original ones if other things happened to be better for his patients because of a difference in the winds or d some other unusual and unexpected act of God? Would the doctor feel it his duty to maintain stubbornly that there must be no transgression of the strict letter of those original prescriptions of his? Would he refuse to issue new prescriptions, or condemn a patient who was venturing to act contrary to the

---

For example, Aristotle in his *Politics* (VI, iii, 1319b37 ff.) states that in providing for the preservation of their states lawgivers should enact unwritten as well as written laws conducive to that end. It is "unwritten law" in this sense which Plato in the *Laws* insists upon as one of the "rivets" of society alongside the statute law: for instance, he makes his rules about the training of infants from birth "unwritten" rules, since it would be ridiculous to formulate them as laws; but they are obviously of first importance (*Laws*, VII, 790a, and especially 793a ff.). [Ed.]

prescriptions he had written out for him in the belief that those former prescriptions were the true canons of medicine and of health, and that therefore all contravention of them must lead to disease and be contrary to medical science? Surely any such claims, in circumstances where a science is involved and a true art is at work, would only make all such prescrip- e tions supremely ridiculous.

Y.S. Yes, it would indeed.

Str. Imagine, then, the case of a scientific legislator. Suppose that by a written code or by unwritten legislation he has laid down what is just and unjust, honorable and disgraceful, good and bad for the several communities of the human flock who live in their cities as their appointed pasture, shepherded by the codes their legislators have provided. If this man, who drew up his code with the help of his art, wishes to amend it, or if another scientific legislator of this kind appears on the scene, will these be forbidden to enact new laws differing from the 296 earlier ones? Surely such a prohibition would in truth appear as ridiculous in the case of the legislator as it was in the case of the doctor, would it not?

Y.S. Of course.

Str. But are you familiar with the argument one usually hears advanced when an issue like this is raised?

Y.S. No, I cannot remember it at the moment, at any rate.

Str. It is quite a plausible argument, I grant. They contend that if a man discovers better laws than those already enacted he must in every instance first persuade his own city to accept them before he can have them passed.

Y.S. But what of this? Surely this is a sound contention.

Str. It may be. But answer this question. Suppose a man b fails to persuade his city and forces his better laws upon it, what name are we to apply to force so used? But no, do not answer that question yet, for there are others about our previous discussion to be answered first.

Y.S. What are they?

Str. Suppose that the doctor of whom we spoke fails to persuade the patient but has a mastery of medical knowledge;

and suppose that he forces a particular course of treatment which goes against written prescription but is actually more salutary on a child patient, maybe, or on a man or a woman. What are we to call force of this kind? Whatever we decide to call it, we shall not call it "an offense against the art of medicine" or "a breach of the laws of health." Surely the very last thing a patient who is so constrained is entitled to say is that c the doctor's act in applying the constraint was contrary to the art of medicine and an aggravation of his disease.

Y.S. You are quite right.

Str. By what name, then, do we call an offense against the art of statesmanship? Would it not be called dishonor, vice, injustice?

Y.S. Assuredly.

Str. What then shall we say of citizens of a state who have been forced to do things which are contrary to written laws and ancestral customs but are nevertheless more just, effective, and noble than what they did before? How shall we regard d censure by these citizens of the force which has been applied in these circumstances? Unless they wish to appear ridiculous in the extreme, there is one thing they must refrain from saying. They must not assert in any such instance that in being subjected to compulsion they have suffered disgrace, injustice, or evil at the hands of those who compelled them.

Y.S. That is quite true.

Str. Can acts imposed under compulsion be right if the compeller is rich but wrong if he is poor? Surely what matters is that with or without persuasion, rich or poor, according to a e written code or against it, the ruler does what is really beneficial. This ought to be the truest criterion for the proper administration of a state, even if it involves compulsion, the criterion by which a wise and good ruler will administer the affairs of his subjects. The ship's captain fixes his attention on the real welfare at any given time of his ship and his crew. He 297 lays down no written enactments but supplies as a law his knowledge of seamanship to preserve the lives of his shipmates. Would not a true constitution be just like this and work in the same way if the rulers really understood what government is and employed their art as a stronger power for good than any written laws? Rulers with this sound attitude of mind cannot possibly do any wrong so long as they keep firmly to the one great principle, that they must always administer impartial justice to their subjects under the guidance of intelligence and the art of government. Then they will not only b preserve the lives of their subjects but reform their characters too, so far as that can be done.

Y.S. There can be no objection to your last remarks at any rate.

Str. No, nor can there be to what we said earlier, either.

Y.S. To what are you referring?

Str. You remember that we said that in no state whatsoever could it happen that a large number of people received this gift of political wisdom which would enable them to govern the city by the pure intelligence which would accompany it.[25] Only in the hands of a select few or of an individual can we c look for that one true constitution. For we must call all other constitutions mere imitations of this. Some are more perfect copies of it, as we said a little earlier, others are grosser and less adequate imitations.

Y.S. What do you really mean by this? For I must admit that I did not really understand what you said before about these "imitations."

Str. But I must make you understand. It would be a serious failing to start a discussion of this issue and then simply drop it without exposing the error which is rampant today in all that is said about it. d

25 Here and at 292e I have translated πλῆθος as "a large number," not as "the mass" of the people, for though the political implications are present to Plato's mind, he is trying to state what he believes to be a true and scientific fact, which justifies among other things distrust of "the masses." This fact is the limited spread in a community of intelligence trainable in a particular art. You do not find a large number of potential doctors, shoemakers, pilots, etc., in a given society: why should you find *a large number* of potential statesmen? Only statesmen should govern, just as only pilots should steer.

Y.S. And what is this error?

Str. That is what we must now seek out, though it involves a search over unfamiliar ground and the error is hard to discover. We may say, then, that there is only one constitution in the true sense—the one we have described. For the rest of them owe their very preservation to their following the written code of laws enacted for this true state and to a strict adherence to a rule which we now admit to be desirable though it falls short of the ideal.

Y.S. What rule is this?

Str. The rule that none of the citizens may venture to do e any act contrary to the laws, and that if any of them ventures to do such act, the penalty is to be death, and all the most severe penalties. This is the most correct and most desirable course as a second-best when the ideal we have just described has been set aside. We must now go on to say how this state of affairs we have just called second-best is achieved in practice, must we not?

Y.S. Yes, we must.

Str. Let us go back once again to the images with which we have constantly to compare the ruler who really is a kingly ruler.

Y.S. What images?

Str. The worthy ship's captain and the doctor "worth a dozen other men." [26] Let us picture to ourselves a situation in which they might find themselves and see how it all works out in their case.

Y.S. What situation?

298 *Str.* Suppose we all suddenly reflected that we are exposed to them in a most terrifying way. Every doctor, you see, can

[26] The reference is to the *Iliad* (XI, 514). Paris wounds Machaon, "the noble leech, son of Asclepius," in the fight and the Greeks are full of anxiety for his life, since "a leech is worth many other men," and so Nestor drives him to safety from the battle to the Greek ships.

The "worthy ship's captain" may imply reference to an extensive parallel passage at *Republic,* VI, 488a ff., but the "ship of state," one of the oldest Greek metaphors, goes back at least to Alcaeus (600 B.C.). The *risk* of navigating is always in mind.

preserve the life of any he will among us, and can hurt any he will by knife or cautery or by demanding fees which are nothing but imposed taxes—for only the tiniest proportion of them is spent on the patient and all the rest goes to keep the doctor and his household. Their final enormity is to accept bribes from the patient's relations or from his enemies and put him b to death. Ships' captains perform countless deeds of a similar kind. They will enter into a conspiracy to put out to sea with you and then leave you stranded, or else they will create disasters on the high sea and throw the passengers overboard—and these are not all their misdeeds. Suppose we formed this view of doctors and captains and then framed the following resolution about them:

" I. Neither medicine nor seamanship may be entrusted in future with absolute control in its particular sphere, either c over slaves or over free citizens.

" II. We therefore resolve to gather together an assembly either of the whole people or of the wealthy alone.[27]

"III. It shall be lawful for laymen and men of any calling at all to advise this assembly on seamanship and medicine; that is to say:

" (a) on the drugs and surgical instruments appropriate to the treatment of the sick;

" (b) on ships and their tackle, on the handling of vessels d and on perils of the sea, including

" (i) risks arising from wind and tide;

" (ii) risks arising from encountering pirates;

" (iii) risks arising from maneuvering of warships against enemy warships in the event of a naval engagement."

This decree of the assembly of the people (whether based on the advice of a few doctors and sailors or on the advice of many unqualified people) is to be inscribed on tablets of wood

27 Here we have recognized the possibility of an oligarchic assembly based on a census of wealth and not of knowledge of the facts, and it is as unreasonable in Plato's view as a democratic assembly containing all the citizens. However, the latter—and Athens, of course, in particular—is his real target and at 298d *fin.* he forgets about the oligarchic alternative and thinks only of Athens. But this alternative reappears at 298e.

and of stone,[28] and some of the rules so resolved upon are ordained as unwritten ancestral customs. Forever thereafter medicine and navigation may only be practiced according to these laws and customs.

e

Y.S. A pretty state of affairs this!

Str. But we have not done yet. Suppose that they resolve further to appoint magistrates chosen by lot annually either from among the wealthy or from all citizens. Some of these magistrates, once they are appointed, are to take command of ships and navigate them, and others are to cure the sick according to the written code.

Y.S. This is getting worse!

Str. But we have not done—see what follows. When the year of office of each of these magistrates expires, a court must be established consisting either of wealthy citizens on the basis of a preceding selection,[29] or by lot, perhaps from the people

[28] The laws of Solon were inscribed on three-sided wooden blocks turning on a pivot called *kyrbeis;* these are specifically referred to here. The laws were later transferred to plaques of marble or bronze called *stelai.* These were in use in the fourth century at Athens.

[29] The reference seems to be to the provision in the Solonian constitution for choosing magistrates (Aristotle, *Constitution of Athens,* 8, 1) and in particular for choosing archons. Ten men were selected openly by each of the four tribes from themselves and nine of these forty were selected by lot to be archons. All magistracies were confined to the three highest property-classes and the archonship was probably limited to the wealthiest class. In his discussion of the Solonian constitution in the *Politics* (II, xii), Aristotle notes this as an aristocratic element in it. Though this πρόκρισις had given way by the fourth century to a double sortition of those ready to stand for office from all classes, a reference by Demosthenes (LVII, 46) to his personal "selection" for a priesthood (which he gives as a proof of his social standing) suggests that the method persisted for certain purposes. Some magistrates are to be so selected, according to Plato in the *Laws* (XII, 945b).

It is important to note, however, that the immediate reference here is to a jury which is to audit the work of the magistrate. Solon opened the jury-courts to the whole people—his most "democratic" act, which was of fundamental importance. How then, it will be asked, can the Solonian πρόκρισις be in question here, where jurymen and not magistrates are concerned?

No doubt πρόκρισις might be an element in an oligarchic constitution,

as a whole. The magistrates are to be summoned before these men and to be subjected to audit. It is open to anyone to lay an accusation against them that during their year of office they failed to sail the ships according to the written laws or the ancient custom of our forebears. Similar charges may be brought concerning the healers of the sick. If the verdict goes against any of them, the court must assess the penalty or the fine which the convicted parties must pay. 299

Y.S. Well, then, the man who took office voluntarily in such a society would deserve any punishment and any fine that might be imposed. b

Str. Then there can be further misdemeanors, and we must enact a law to provide against them. If a man be found guilty of inquiry into piloting and seamanship, health and, in medicine, the truth about the influence of hot and cold winds in contravention of this written law, and if he be guilty of airing any theories of his own on such things, action must be taken to suppress him. First we must deny him the title of "doctor" or "captain." Instead we must call him a man with his head in the clouds, one of these chattering sophists. Furthermore, it will be lawful for any citizen so desiring to indict him before a court of justice (or what passes for such a court) on the charge of corrupting the younger men and influencing them to go in for seamanship and medicine in an illegal manner by exercising an absolute rule over ships and patients. If he is found guilty of influencing young or old against the laws and written enactments, he shall suffer the utmost penalties. For there must be no wisdom greater than the wisdom of the laws. No one c

---

and a reference here to an existing constitution in which jurymen were so selected is quite possible. But is it not more likely that Plato is tilting at contemporary "constitutionalists" at Athens who wanted to restore "the ancestral constitution"? Isocrates was to point to this element of "selection of the best" in his *Areopagiticus,* 22, a few years later. May it not have been a serious proposition by the "moderates" at the time—a way of stopping the rot caused by complete democratic control of the courts? If so, Plato's answer is, "The rot goes deeper than this and affects 'Solonian' democracy as much as any other."

need be ignorant of medicine and health, or of piloting and seamanship. The laws are there written out for our conning, d the ancient customs are firmly established in our midst. Any who really desire to learn may learn.

Suppose, Socrates, that all the sciences are treated like this. How do you imagine that generalship and hunting in all their forms would be affected? What would happen to painting and other representational arts, or to building and manufacture of all types of implements under such conditions; and how could farming or any cultivation whatever be carried on? Imagine the rearing of horses and other animals tied down to written prescription, or divination, or any ancillary functions so con- e trolled. What would legally governed draughts be like, or legal mathematics, whether simple arithmetic, plane geometry, stereometry, or kinematics?[30] What would the world be like if everything worked on this principle, organized throughout according to written laws and not according to the relevant arts?

Y.S. It is quite clear that the arts would all be annihilated and that they could never be resurrected because of this law which forbids all research. The result would be that life, which is hard enough as it is, would be quite impossible then and not worth living.

300 *Str.* Yes, but there is a further possible degradation to consider. Suppose we compel each of these arts to function according to a written code and place a magistrate in charge of this code either by election or by the fall of the lot. Suppose

[30] The reference here, as at 284e, is to the four stages of the mathematical curriculum of the Academy, which are represented in the *Republic* as the course of higher education for the philosopher-king prescribed in Book VII. The progress from arithmetic to kinematics (the movements of bodies having three dimensions, as the *Republic* more simply calls it) is in a sense a progress to greater "abstraction" since the problems at each stage have to be more generally stated, but in another sense it is an approach to the intellectual comprehension of all sense data and their behavior and it leads finally to an appreciation of the laws behind astronomical phenomena. It is this mathematical "intellectual" astronomy, as distinct from "almanac" work, which leads sense-bound man up to philosophical truth and a knowledge of the reason embodied in the "heavens" (see *Timaeus,* 47a ff.).

then that he has no regard for the written code and, from motives of personal profit and favoritism, embarks on a course contrary to law, without any knowledge. Evil as the former state was, will not this latter one be still worse?

Y.S. It will indeed.

Str. The laws which have been laid down represent the fruit of long experience—one must admit that. Each of them incorporates the clever advice of some counselor who has persuaded the public assembly to enact it. Any man who dares by his action to infringe these laws is guilty of a wrong many times greater than the wrong done by strict laws, for such transgression, if tolerated, would do even more than a written code to pervert all ordered activity. b

Y.S. Yes, of course it would.

Str. Then so long as men enact laws and written codes governing any department of life, our second-best method of government is to forbid any individual or any group to perform any act in contravention of these laws. c

Y.S. True.

Str. Then laws would seem to be written copies of scientific truth in the various departments of life they cover, copies based as far as possible on the instructions received from those who really possess the scientific truth on these matters.

Y.S. Yes, of course.

Str. And yet we must never lose sight of the truth we stated before. The man with the real knowledge, the true statesman, will in many instances allow his activities to be dictated by his art and pay no regard to written prescriptions. He will do this whenever he is convinced that there are other measures which are better than the instructions he previously wrote and sent to people at a time when he could not be there to control them personally. d

Y.S. Yes, that was what we said.

Str. So any individual or any group who possess a code of laws but try to introduce some change in them because they consider it an improvement are doing the same thing according to their lights as the true statesman.

Y.S. Yes.

Str. But if they acted like this with minds unenlightened by knowledge, they would indeed try to copy the true original, but would copy it very badly. If on the other hand they pos- e sessed scientific knowledge, it would no longer be a case of copying at all; it would be the real and original truth we are talking about.

Y.S. Certainly.

Str. Now it has been argued already and we have agreed that no large group of men is capable of acquiring any art, be it what you will.

Y.S. That stands as our agreed conclusion.

9. *Digression on the Imitative Constitutions* (300e-303b)

Str. Granted then, that an art of kingly rule exists, the wealthy group or the whole citizen body would never be able to acquire this science of statesmanship.

Y.S. How could they?

Str. It seems to follow that there is an invariable rule which these imitative constitutions must obey if they mean to repro- 301 duce as far as they can that one true constitution, which is government by the one real statesman using real statecraft. They must all keep strictly to the laws once they have been laid down and never transgress written enactments and established, ancestral customs.

Y.S. Quite right.

Str. When the wealthy seek to copy the ideal constitution we call the constitution which results "aristocracy," but when they disregard the laws, the constitution produced is "oligarchy."

Y.S. I suppose so.

Str. But when one individual governs according to laws, b imitating the truly wise ruler, we call him "king." We make no difference in name between the individual ruler guided by scientific knowledge and the individual ruler guided by opinion and acting according to the laws.

Y.S. That seems to be so.

Str. And so if there really were an example of a truly wise ruler in power his name would undoubtedly be the same—"the king"; it could not be anything else. So the total of the names of the constitutions now under consideration comes to five only.[31]

Y.S. So it seems.

Str. But stay, what of the case where one man rules but does not govern his actions either by laws or by ancient customs, but claims falsely what only the truly wise ruler had a right to claim, and says that the best course must be taken in defiance of written codes? If in fact it is only his passion and his ignorance that lead him to attempt to copy the true statesman, must we not call him and all like him by the name of tyrant? c

[31] The passage takes up the thread laid aside at 292a. At 291d *fin.* we are told that the three main types have produced two further subtypes to make the total five—monarchy, tyranny, aristocracy, oligarchy, democracy. This we have seen (see note 23, p. 62) to be the formal Academy "division," and this corroborates the reading of the present passage which I have adopted here. We have here an expansion of five to seven, since the name "monarchy" or "kingship" covers two types, and so does "democracy." Plato counts up the five names for us himself at 301c *fin.* But he goes on to one more lesson on the danger of relying on names rather than things (i.e., real kinds). More scientific analysis provides the new total—seven—at 302c. Democracy is divided into two like the other main types, and the rule of the true statesman is distinguished from them all (and in particular from law-abiding monarchy), so that a final classification is reached and may be tabulated as follows:

THE SEVEN CONSTITUTIONS

A. *Imitative*			
I. Rule of one man:	(*a*)	monarchy	1
	(*b*)	tyranny	2
II. Rule of a few men:	(*a*)	aristocracy	3
	(*b*)	oligarchy	4
III. Rule of many:	(*a*)	democracy	5
	(*b*)	democracy	6
B. *Genuine*			
Rule of true statesman	(*c*)		7

(*a*) = law-abiding constitution, (*b*) = constitution flouting law, (*c*) = constitution above all laws.

Y.S. Unquestionably.

Str. So then we have the tyrant and the king, then oligarchy and aristocracy, then democracy, all of which arise when men turn down the idea of the one true and scientific ruler. Men doubt whether any man will ever be found fit to exercise such

d perfect rule as to be willing and able to rule with moral and intellectual insight and to render every man what is his due according to divine and human law with strict fairness. They feel sure that a man with such absolute power will be bound to employ it to the hurt and injury and death of anyone he pleases. But it remains true that if the kind of ruler we have described were to appear on earth he would be acclaimed, and he would spend his days guiding in perfect felicity that one and only true commonwealth worthy of the name.

Y.S. That is so, of course.

Str. We must take things as they are, however, and kings do

e not arise in cities in the natural course of things in the way the royal bee is born in a beehive—one individual obviously outstanding in body and mind.[32] And therefore it seems men have to gather together and work out written codes, chasing to catch the tracks of the true constitution.

Y.S. So it would seem.

Str. Is it surprising, Socrates, that under these constitutions of ours hosts of ills have arisen and more must be expected in the future? They all rest on the sandy foundation of action according to law and custom without real scientific knowledge.

302 Another art that worked on such a foundation would obviously ruin all that it sought to build up. But what is even more surprising is the sheer native strength a city possesses nevertheless. For all our cities, as we know, have now been subject to such ills for an infinite length of time, and yet some of them have not come to ruin but still stand firm. However,

[32] This may be a direct reference to Xenophon, *Cyropaedeia,* V, i, 24, where Artabazus is made to compare Cyrus to the leader of the bees, whom they follow willingly because of his undoubted physical superiority. The Greeks spoke of the "king" bee, not of the "queen" bee, though Aristotle recognizes the existence of the view that the leader is a queen and Xenophon, *Oeconomicus,* vii, 32, exhorts his wife to emulate her.

we see many instances of cities going down like sinking ships to their destruction. There have been such wrecks in the past and there surely will be others in the future, caused by the worthlessness of captains and crews alike. For these are guilty of supreme ignorance of what matters most. They are men who know little or nothing of real political truth and yet they consider themselves to know it from end to end and suppose that they are better instructed in this science than in any other. b

Y.S. Very true.

Str. All these imperfect constitutions are difficult to live under, but we might ask ourselves which of them is hardest to bear and which is most tolerable. Ought we perhaps to examine this matter, though it is not directly relevant to our present purpose? After all, one must remember that, speaking quite generally, the aim of all the actions of men everywhere is to secure for themselves the most tolerable life they can.[33]

Y.S. Then we can hardly help considering the question.

Str. There is one of three constitutions which you must regard as being at once the hardest to live under and the easiest. c

Y.S. How do you mean?

Str. I just want to remind you that at the beginning of this footnote to our discussion we enumerated three constitutions —the rule of one, the rule of the few, and the rule of the many.[34]

33 This general statement that all men seek the most tolerable living conditions is a notable one. It suggests that the Epicurean ideal of freedom from trouble had support in Athens before Epicurus appeared and that this ideal could be held quite apart from the Epicurean theory of the nature of the physical universe. Clement of Alexandria tells us that Speusippus (Plato's nephew and successor) believed that all men pursue settled happiness and that the good aim at undisturbedness. Aristotle's reference to *ἀπάθεια* in *Eth. Nic.*, II, iii, 1104b, 24, probably points to this form of the ideal rather than to a Stoic form of apathy.

The view that all men seek a good "uncertain in their grasp of what it is but divining it to be some real thing" is, of course, stated in the *Republic* itself (VI, 505d ff.) but the view that this good can be pleasure is scouted there. Here the natural search of unenlightened humanity for "a quiet life" is treated more sympathetically.

34 The three types of constitution were in fact named as far back as

Y.S. We did.

Str. Dividing each of three into two, let us make six, having first separated the true constitution from all, calling it the seventh.

Y.S. How shall we divide the three others?

d *Str.* Under the rule of one we get kingly rule and tyranny; under the rule of the few, as we said, come the auspicious forms of it, aristocracy, and also oligarchy. As for the subdivisions of the rule of the many, though we gave both forms of it one name previously, democracy, we must now treat it as twofold.

Y.S. How is this? How can it be divided?

Str. By the same division as the others, even though the e word "democracy" proves to be doing double duty. Rule according to law and rule in defiance of law is as possible under democracy as under the other constitutions.

Y.S. Yes, it is.

Str. This division of democracy into two kinds was not serviceable previously, as we indicated at the time; for we were seeking then to define a perfect constitution. Now, however, we have excluded the perfect constitution from our reckoning and have before us those that have to serve us as constitutions in default of it. In this group we find the principle of obedience to law or contravention of law dividing each type of rule into two types.[35]

291d, though the discussion on their relative merits, which is more strictly the "footnote," only begins at 302b. In a sense the strict classification of the "imitative" constitutions is relevant to the main theme since the several rulers in them have all to be distinguished from the true statesman, as Plato goes on to say (303c).

[35] This completes the very important point made at 292c, d. The various *differentiae* mentioned there (riches or poverty, persuasion or violence) are abandoned, but the *differentia* "obeying or contravening the law" is said here to be a true and necessary *differentia* in the case of the three pairs of imitative constitutions. The argument from 292b onwards shows that there is no such *differentia* within the rule of the true statesman: he may rule according to or contrary to the laws and yet be a true statesman. But the three types of constitutions, as they were commonly distinguished by the Greeks, divide into six on this principle (see the

Y.S. So it seems from the argument that was put forward just now.

Str. The rule of one man, if it has been kept within bounds by the written rules we call laws, is the best of all the six; but when it is lawless it is hard, and the most grievous to have to live with.

303 *Y.S.* So it would seem.

Str. As for the rule of a few, just as the few constitute a middle term between the one and the many, so we must regard the rule of the few as of middle potency for good or ill. The rule of the many is weak in every way; it is not capable of any real good or of any serious evil as compared with the other two. This is because in a democracy sovereignty has been divided out in small portions among a large number of rulers. Therefore, of all three constitutions that are law-abiding, democracy is the worst; but of the three that flout the laws, democracy is the best. Thus if all constitutions are unprincipled the best thing to do is to live in a democracy. But when con- b stitutions are well ordered, democracy is the least desirable, and monarchy, the first of the six, is by far the best to live under—unless of course the seventh is possible, for that must always be exalted, like a god among mortals, above all other constitutions.

Y.S. Things do seem to work out in this way, and so we must act as you say.

10. Return to the Final Definition (303b-311c)

Str. Therefore all who take part in one of these governments—apart from the one based on real knowledge—are to be c distinguished from the true statesman. They are not statesmen; they are party leaders, leaders of bogus governments and them-

table at the end of note 31, p. 79). Probably Plato also regards persuasion and violence as accompanying law and lawlessness respectively. The true statesman may use curative violence (292c) but illegal violence is inadmissible elsewhere. The law persuades and only penalizes as a last resort by common consent. King and tyrant are distinguished on this principle at 276d above.

selves as bogus as their systems. The supreme imitators and tricksters, they are of all sophists the archsophists.

Y.S. The wheel seems to have come full circle, now that the title of sophist goes to those who most deserve it, to the so-called politicians.

Str. So this fantastic pageant that seemed like some strange masque of centaurs or some band of satyrs stands revealed for what it is. At much pains we have succeeded at last in distin-
d guishing them and setting them apart, as we must, from all true practice of statesmanship.[36]

Y.S. So we see.

(f) Distinguished from Orators, Generals, and Judges (303d-305e)

Str. There remains another task, and it is even more difficult because the class to be set apart is closer akin to the kingly ruler and also harder to discern clearly. It seems to me that we have reached a point where we have to act like gold-refiners.

Y.S. How so?

Str. We are told that at the first stage of their work the workers separate off earth and stones and much else from the ore. When these are gone there still remain those precious
e substances akin to gold which are so combined with it as to be separable only by fire; I mean bronze and silver and sometimes adamant as well. These are removed only with difficulty as the metal is tried in the refining fire until at last the process yields the sight of unalloyed gold separated off by itself.[37]

[36] The deliberate reference back to 291b emphasizes the return to the main task of definition.

[37] The meaning of "adamant" is uncertain, but it seems clear that the word is used in the same sense here as it is at *Timaeus,* 59b. The "adamant" of Hesiod (*Works and Days,* 147, *Shield,* 137, 231, *Theogony,* 161, 188, 239), which also bound Prometheus (Aeschylus, *Prometheus Bound,* 6), is called gray and pale, and may have been steel. The word "adamant" was used of diamond by Theophrastus not much later than Plato wrote, but this is not likely to be meant here, for the "bud of gold" of which the *Timaeus* speaks in a connection similar to the present one was dark in color, and may be haematite.

The word translated "unalloyed" has wide poetic usage, and "un-

Y.S. Yes, they do say that refining is done like that.

Str. It looks as though we are in a like situation. We have separated from statesmanship the elements which are different, foreign, and repugnant to it; but there still remain the precious elements which are akin to it. These include the art of generalship, the art of administering justice, and that department of the art of public speaking which is closely allied to the kingly art, because it persuades men to do what is right and therefore takes its share in controlling what goes on in a state. How can we best separate these arts also from statesmanship and so bring out the nature of the statesman unalloyed in his essential character? That, after all, is our present object. 304

Y.S. Clearly we must make the attempt by one means or another.

Str. If trying will do it, he shall be shown in his true character. Music will provide us with an example which will help us in our task. I will begin by putting a question to you.

Y.S. What is it?

Str. There is such a thing as learning music or the principles of the handicrafts, is there not? b

Y.S. Yes.

Str. And further: shall we maintain that there is a higher order of science that decides which particular art we ought to learn and which not?

Y.S. Yes, we shall.

Str. We must also agree then that it is different from all the other arts and sciences.

Y.S. Yes.

Str. Ought there to be no priority at all as between these two orders of science? On the other hand, if there is to be priority, must the lower order control the higher or the higher guide and control all the others? c

Y.S. The higher order should control the lower.

Str. Your decision is then that the science which decides

---

sullied gold" may be a quotation; on the other hand, it may well be that it is used here in the literal "trade" sense.

whether we ought to learn a skill or not should have control of the science which actually teaches us that skill.

Y.S. Yes, certainly.

Str. Then in the same way the science which decides whether persuasion should or should not be used ought to control the operation of the knowledge of persuasion itself.

Y.S. Undoubtedly.

Str. Which is the science to which we must assign the task of persuading the general mass of the population by telling d them imaginative stories rather than by giving them formal instruction?

Y.S. I should say that it is obvious that this is the province to be assigned to rhetoric.[38]

Str. But to which science must we assign the function of deciding whether in any particular situation we must proceed by persuasion, or by coercive measures against a group of men, or whether it is right to take no action at all?

Y.S. The science which can teach us how to decide that will be that which controls the science of persuading and public speaking.

[38] There are three stages in Plato's treatment of rhetoric, which may be briefly noted:

(i) In the *Gorgias* rhetoric, though it claims to be "*the* art," is dismissed as no art at all but only a "knack" and a bogus substitute for true political art.

(ii) In the *Phaedrus* this estimate of the self-styled "art" remains, but we are told that there can nevertheless be a real rhetorical art. It can be practiced by the dialectical philosopher. His dialectic gives him a grasp of truth and a knowledge of what is really like and unlike. Having this knowledge of reality he must proceed to a study of the human soul and of the ways of persuading it. He will then be able to practice the true rhetoric, presenting the metaphysical truth in a form in which it can be acceptable to the unmetaphysical.

(iii) Here in the *Statesman* the positive view of the *Phaedrus* that the art exists is assumed, but the practice of rhetoric is made strictly subordinate and it seems as though someone other than the statesman is to practice it. Would this "someone" be a dialectical philosopher? Would he even be the "qualified adviser" who is as good as a king (see 259a and 293a)? But if so, he would have to limit himself in its use. The orator practically becomes a "government spokesman."

Str. This activity can be none other than the work of the statesman, I suggest.

Y.S. Excellent! That is exactly what it is.

Str. Rhetoric, it seems, has been quickly set apart from statesmanship. It is distinct from statesmanship and yet its e auxiliary.

Y.S. Yes.

Str. Now we must consider the working of another science.

Y.S. Which is that?

Str. Consider the making of decisions on military strategy once war has been declared. What shall we say about this? Is such decision governed by no art at all, or shall we say that there is an art involved here?

Y.S. How could we dream of saying that no art is concerned? Surely generalship and the whole science of warfare operates precisely in this field.

Str. But which is the science which possesses the knowledge and capacity to form a reasoned decision whether to fight or settle a dispute on friendly terms? Is this the work of generalship or does it belong to another?

Y.S. Consistency to our earlier argument requires us to say that it is a different one.

Str. So if our views here are to be consistent with our earlier views on the place of rhetoric, we must decide that this other 305 science controls generalship.

Y.S. I agree.

Str. What science can we attempt to enthrone as queen over that mighty and dreadful art, the art of war in all its range, except the art of truly royal rule?

Y.S. None other.

Str. Then we must not describe the science that generals practice as statesmanship, for it proves to be but a servant of statesmanship.

Y.S. Apparently that is so.

Str. Now turn to another science and let us consider the activity of judges who make straight judgments. b

Y.S. By all means.

Str. Does its province extend beyond the sphere of mutual contractual obligations? It has to act in this sphere by judging what is just or unjust according to the standards set up for it and embodied in the legal rules which it has received from the kingly lawgiver. It shows its peculiar virtue by coming to an impartial decision on the conflicting claims it examines, by refusing to pervert the lawgiver's ordinance through yielding to
c bribery or threats or sentimental appeals, and by rising above all considerations of personal friendship or enmity.

Y.S. Yes, that is so. What you have given us is a correct account of his function and of his duty.

Str. We find, then, that the power of the judges is not a kingly power. The judge guards the law and serves the king.

Y.S. So it would seem.

Str. If you will view all the sciences we have spoken of as a group, you will be bound to see that none of them has turned out to be the science of statesmanship. This is because it is not
d the province of the real kingly science to act on its own, but rather to control the sciences whose natural capacity is to act, inasmuch as it knows the right and the wrong moment for initiating and setting in motion the most important matters in the state. The other sciences must do what they are bidden.

Y.S. Precisely so.

Str. Therefore the sciences we have just treated in detail may not control one another. They may not even control themselves, in fact. Each has its special field of action and each is entitled to the name which designates its proper sphere.[39]

e *Y.S.* So it would seem.

Str. There is a science which controls them all. It is concerned with the laws and with all that belongs to the life of the state. It weaves all into its unified fabric[40] with perfect

[39] That is to say, these three are real sciences of community life but with limited scope—they are not sham sciences like those of the "party leaders" we have dismissed.

[40] The return to weaving is indicated skillfully by the use of this phrase. In the rest of the dialogue the manner of this "weaving" is worked out in detail.

skill. It is a universal science and so we call it by a name of universal scope. That name is one to which I believe this science has the justest claim, the name of "statesmanship."

Y.S. Yes, I agree absolutely.

(g) Weaving the Web of the Human Political Community (305e-311c)

Str. Now that all the classes of sciences active in the government of the state have been distinguished, shall we go on to scrutinize statesmanship on the basis of the art of weaving which provides our example for it?

Y.S. Most certainly.

Str. Then, it seems, we must describe the kingly weaving process. What is it like? How is it done? What is the fabric that results from its labors? 306

Y.S. Obviously.

Str. The task of finding the answers is hard, but we cannot shirk it.

Y.S. No, we must find them at all costs.

Str. To say that one particular part of goodness or virtue clashes with goodness as a whole is to preach a doctrine which is an easy target for the disputatious who appeal to commonly accepted opinion.[41]

41 We are prepared very carefully for a statement which is

(*a*) dramatically impossible in a dialogue supposed to take place in 399 B.C. in which Socrates is a speaker, and

(*b*) a denial of an important tenet of the Academy itself at an earlier time.

We are told at once that we have to run the risk of playing into the hands of outside detractors who deny this Socratic and Platonic tenet of the unity of virtue. The great Protagoras is represented as contending that courage differs from the rest of the virtues though the rest may be treated as one. Socrates confutes this on his own principles (*Protagoras,* 349b ff.). The Socratic position is stated in full in the *Laches.* But the detractors in mind here would not be of the stature of Protagoras. The *Dissoi Logoi* do not contain a chapter on the unity of virtue, but one can easily imagine the kind of chapter it would have been; and discussion at such a level of the Socratic and Platonic doctrines is what is glanced at

Y.S. I do not follow you.

Str. Then let me put the matter in this way. You regard b courage as one part of virtue, I suppose.

Y.S. Surely.

Str. Self-control differs from courage but is a specific part of goodness, just as courage is.

Y.S. Yes.

Str. We have now to be daring and make a startling statement about these two virtues.

Y.S. What is it?

Str. This pair of virtues are in a certain sense enemies, ranged in opposition to each other in many realms of life.

Y.S. What do you mean?

Str. This is not a familiar doctrine by any means. I suppose c that the usual statement is that all the several parts of goodness are in mutual accord.[42]

Y.S. Yes.

Str. Then we must give our very special attention to the matter. Is the position quite so simple as that? Is there not, on the contrary, something inherent in them which keeps alive a family quarrel among them?

---

here. There may also be a reference to popular views that certain characteristic virtues belong to different nations or different cities, and that these distinctive qualities are necessarily antagonistic—Attic wisdom and Spartan phlegm, for instance.

[42] The accord of the several virtues in δικαιοσύνη or righteousness is, of course, the cardinal doctrine in accordance with which the life of the community and the individual is worked out in the first half of the *Republic*. Courage is the particular virtue of the warrior class, but it exists in every individual (429c ff., 442b ff.) and the true self-control is consent to be controlled by reason which has courage as its executive and ally. The *Republic* does indeed promise a further discussion of courage (430c, 16) but it is not reached.

We now make what seems a frontal attack on this position—and though it leads to a new "synthesis" in the sense of the interweaving of the opposing characters, the new statement must necessarily destroy the psychological scheme of the *Republic*. It is equivalent to declaring eternal conflict between the warrior and civilian classes.

Y.S. Certainly we must consider this. Please tell us how we are to do so.

Str. We must consider instances drawn from any and every thing which we regard as excellent and yet classify as mutually opposed.

Y.S. Please explain still more clearly.

Str. Take keenness and speed as an instance—keenness and speed of mind or body, or range in a voice.[43] Such keenness may be seen in an actual living person or it may be represented in music or painting. Have you ever praised examples of these qualities yourself or listened with approval when one of your friends praised them? d

Y.S. Yes.

Str. Do you happen to remember the way in which the approval is expressed in all these instances?

Y.S. No.

Str. I wonder if I could really manage to put my thoughts on the subject into words and make them clear to you.

Y.S. I am sure you could. e

Str. You seem to think it a light task! However, let us see the principle at work in those mutually opposite classes. We admire speed and intensity and keenness in many forms of action and under all kinds of circumstances. But whether the keenness of mind or body or the pitch of the voice is admired, we always find ourselves using one word to praise it—the word "vigorous."

[43] We are told in the *Timaeus* (at 67b) that a rapid vibration (or more strictly a quick succession of blows inflicted on the air by the source of sound) gives a high note, and the slower the original motion, the lower the pitch. Aristotle has the same explanation in principle (*De Anima*, 420a, 30) but scruples to call a "high" note "quick." It is unfortunate for a translator that Plato did not share this scruple; for this inclusion of "speed" of voice with other kinds of speed makes it almost impossible to find a common English epithet. With the "slow" voice, which we call "low," the problem is even worse. I have done the best I could by employing "vigorous" and "controlled," though I am aware that baritones can be vigorous and sopranos controlled.

Y.S. How so?

Str. "That is keen and vigorous," we say in the first instance; in another case, "That is speedy and vigorous," or in yet another case, "That is intense and vigorous." In all the instances we use this epithet "vigorous" as applying in common to the people or things concerned, in order to express our approval of this quality in them.

Y.S. True.

Str. On the other hand, do we not quite often find ourselves 307 approving gentleness and quietness as we meet it in many kinds of human actions?

Y.S. Yes, very decidedly.[44]

Str. Do we not describe this behavior by using an epithet which is the exact opposite of "vigorous," which was the term we applied to the other group of things?

Y.S. How do you mean?

Str. We constantly admire quietness and self-control in processes of restrained thinking, in deliberate and gentle deeds, in a smooth deep voice, in all steady rhythmic movement, or in b suitable restraint in artistic representation. Whenever we express such approval do we not use the expression "controlled" to describe all these excellences rather than "vigorous"?

Y.S. Very true.

Str. But when we find either of these kinds of behavior appearing out of its due time, we have different names for each of them and in that case we express our censure by attributing to them quite contrary qualities through the names we use.

Y.S. How so?

Str. When keenness, speed, and persistence turn out to be unseasonably excessive, we call it "wanton" and "mad." Un- c seasonable heaviness, slowness, or softness we call "cowardly" or "indolent." One can generalize further. The very natures of

[44] Quiet behavior is put forward by Charmides as the essence of self-control, and though this is not enough for Socrates, it does represent the better-class Athenian ideal of good manners in the young. These are described nostalgically by Isocrates. (See Plato, *Charmides*, 159b; *Republic*, 425a; Isocrates, *Areopagiticus*, 48, 49.)

vigor and self-control are ranged in mutual exclusiveness and in opposition to each other; it is not simply a case of conflict between these particular manifestations of them. They never meet in the activities of life without causing conflicts, and if we pursue the matter further, we shall see that people whose minds come to be dominated by either of them are in conflict with one another.

Y.S. In what sphere do these conflicts occur?

Str. In all the things we have just considered, of course, but in many others too, I think. Men react to situations in one way d or another according to the affinities of their own dispositions. They favor some forms of action as being akin to their own character, and they disparage acts arising from opposite tendencies as being foreign to themselves. Thus men come into violent conflict with one another on many issues.

Y.S. Yes, they seem to do so.

Str. Considered as a conflict of different types, this is a mere trifle; but when the conflict arises over matters of high public importance it becomes the most inimical of all the plagues which can threaten the life of a state.

Y.S. What kind of evils do you mean?

Str. Of course I mean all which concern the organization of e human life. Men who are outstanding in moderation are always ready to lead a quiet life. They want to keep themselves to themselves and to mind their own business. They conduct all their dealings with their fellow citizens on this principle and are prone to take the same line in foreign policy and preserve peace at any price with foreign states. Because of their indulgence of this passion for peace at the wrong times, whenever they are able to carry their policy into effect they become unwarlike themselves without being aware of it and render their young men unwarlike as well. Thus they are always at the mercy of the aggressor, and the result is that within a very few years they and their children and the entire state wake up to find that their freedom is gone and that they are reduced to 308 slavery.

Y.S. You have described a hard and bitter experience.

Str. What, then, is the history of those whose bent is rather toward vigorous and courageous action? Do we not find them forever dragging their cities into war and bringing them up against many powerful foes on all sides just because they love a military existence too fiercely? And what is the result? Either they destroy their country altogether, or else they bring it into slavery and subjection to its enemies.

b *Y.S.* Yes, that is true too.

Str. Can we deny, then, that in these high matters these two types of character are bound to become hostile to one another and so take up opposing party lines?

Y.S. We are bound to admit it.

Str. We have discovered, then, the answer to the question which we raised at the beginning of this conversation. We find that important parts of goodness are at variance with one another and that they set at variance the men in whom they predominate.

Y.S. So it seems.

Str. There is a further point to consider.

Y.S. What is it?

c *Str.* Does any science which works by combining materials deliberately choose to make any of its products, even the least important of them, out of a combination of good material with bad? Does not every science, whatever material it works in, reject bad material as far as possible and use what is good and serviceable? The materials may be alike or dissimilar, but science can combine them to form one product and fashion them to a structure proper to their specific function.

Y.S. Yes.

d *Str.* Surely, then, the true and genuine statesmanship we are concerned with could never choose deliberately to construct any state out of a combination of good and bad men. Obviously it will first put them to the test in games.[45] After this first test it will go on to entrust the young to competent educators who are able to render this particular service, but it will

[45] This is fully developed in the *Laws,* especially at VII, 793e ff., where we have a description of the Platonic nursery school.

retain direction and oversight of them all the time. This is exactly like weaving. The art of weaving hands over the materials it intends to use for the fabric to the carders and others concerned with preparatory processes, and yet it watches their work at every stage, retaining the direction and oversight itself and indicating to each auxiliary art such duties as it deems that each can usefully perform to make ready the threads for its own task of fashioning the web. e

Y.S. Precisely.

Str. This is the way I see the kingly science dealing with those who rear and educate children according to the laws. It keeps the power of direction to itself. The only form of training it will permit is the one by which the educator produces the type of character fitted for its task. It bids the educator encourage the young in these activities and in no others. Some pupils do not have the capacity to have any part in courageous and self-controlled behavior and to acquire the other virtuous tendencies, but are impelled to godlessness and to vaunting pride and injustice by the drive of an evil nature. These the king expels from the community. He puts them to death or banishes them or else he chastises them by the severest public disgrace.[46] 309

[46] This provision is no more extreme than that of *Republic,* IV, 410a. It is, in fact, a little less extreme, in that it suggests exile and social disgrace as alternatives to death in some cases. The passage seems more savage in its severity because of the parallel with weaving—for that implies a mere discarding of ill-wrought strands that cannot be woven into the web. It should, however, be clearly understood that the "liquidation" of the socially intractable was always part of Plato's political theory and it is useless to attempt to deny it, or to ascribe it only to the bitterness of old age. Finding in Plato so high a conception of human nature as such, we tend to expect also the respect for the individual, the tolerance of recalcitrants and the care for the diseased which coexist with that high conception of humanity in the Christian faith. But this is not fair to Plato. Even in *Laws,* X, where there seems to be something similar to the Inquisition's desire to save the heretic's soul before sending him to death, the real purpose is to prevent sacrilege, growth of private shrines and social disruption. The obstinate heretic is to be cast out unburied (*Laws,* X, 909c) and there is no prayer for his soul.

Y.S. So one usually hears it stated.

Str. Furthermore, he reduces those who wallow in ignorance and groveling subservience to the status of slaves.[47]

Y.S. Quite rightly.

Str. The kingly science will then take over all the rest—all
b those who, under the training process, do in fact achieve sufficient nobility of character to stand up to the royal weaving process and yet to submit to it while it combines them all scientifically into a unity. Those in whom courage predominates will be treated as having the firm warplike character, as one might call it. Those who incline to moderation will be used by him for what we may, in terms of our image, call the supple, soft, wooflike strands of the web. It then tries to combine and weave together these two groups, exhibiting their mutually opposed characters in the following manner.[48]

Y.S. How?

c *Str.* It first unites that element in their souls which is eternal by a divine bond, since it is akin to the divine. After this divine bond it will in turn unite their animal nature by human bonds.

Y.S. What do you mean by this?

Str. When there is implanted in the soul of men a right

[47] This suggestion that certain members of the community could be degraded to slavery by reason of their mental and moral deficiency differs from what is said about slavery both in the *Republic* and the *Laws.* It is nearer to what Aristotle says about "slaves by nature" in the *Politics* (*Politics,* I, 5).

[48] Why does Plato find it necessary to insist that the qualities are irreconcilable opposites here? In the *Republic* (IV, 410d, e) we have a very similar analysis of the situation: the Guardians must have courage and self-control. Too much gymnastics (in the Greek sense) leads to wildness, too much music or philosophy to softness, and so the two must be correctly combined. This can be said without upsetting the doctrine of the unity of virtue of the psychological scheme of the *Republic.* The mere opposition of "warp" and "woof" hardly necessitates so radical an opposition of the virtues predominant in each. The reason is perhaps that with his growing disillusionment in the perfectibility of man Plato now no longer believes that these two opposite virtues can exist in the same soul.

opinion concerning what is honorable, just, and good, and what is the opposite of these—an opinion based on absolute truth and settled as an unshakable conviction—I declare that such a conviction is a manifestation of the divine in a race which is of supernatural lineage.[49]

Y.S. It could not be more suitably described.

Str. Do we realize that it is the true statesman, in that he is the good and true lawgiver, who alone is able to forge by the inspiration of the kingly art this bond of true conviction uniting those we have just described, who have profited as they should from their education? d

Y.S. That is certainly as one would expect.

Str. The ruler who cannot weld that bond we will never honor with those glorious titles, "statesman" and "king."

Y.S. Most rightly not.

Str. Well, then, will it not work out like this? The soul full of vigor and courage will be made gentle by its grasp of this truth and nothing else will make it more willing to take part in righteousness. If such a soul refused this gift, it will sink in the scale and become savage like a beast. e

Y.S. True.

Str. What of the moderate soul? Sharing this firm conviction of truth, will it not be truly self-controlled and prudent, or at any rate prudent enough to meet its public duties? But if it refuses to share this conviction, it deserves to be called foolish and our reproach of it is entirely proper.

Y.S. It is indeed.

Str. Do we agree, then, that this interweaving, this linking

[49] The divine bond is "right opinion based on absolute truth which has become settled conviction"—we might say "sound standards and a sense of values." The ordinary citizen could not understand fully the metaphysical ground of such opinion, and yet in accepting it through the laws and education prescribed by the statesman he could achieve a *Lebensphilosophie,* a "faith to live by." This Plato now claims to be an element of the divine in man. He has up to now only said this openly about the highest, god-like, reasoning faculty of the philosopher. The true statesman enables the unphilosophic citizens to achieve their heavenly destiny and realize their heavenly origin so far as they are able.

together, can never be lasting if vicious men are joined with other vicious men or good men with vicious? Surely no science would seriously try to forge such links among such men.

Y.S. How could it?

310 *Str.* But in those characters of noble nature from their earliest days whose nurture too has been all it should be, the laws can foster the growth of this common bond of conviction, and only in these. This is the medicine prescribed for them by science. This most godlike bond alone can unite the elements of goodness which are divers in nature and would else be opposing in tendency.

Y.S. Most true.

Str. There remain the other bonds, the human ones. When one sets to work with the divine link already forged it is not very difficult to see what these are and then to forge them.

b *Y.S.* But what are these links and how can they be forged?

Str. They are forged by establishing intermarriage between the two types so that the children of the mixed marriages are, so to speak, shared between them, and by restricting private arrangements for marrying off daughters. Most men make unsuitable matches from the point of view of begetting children of the best type of character.

Y.S. What do you mean?

Str. Would anyone seriously think it worthwhile to censure in any respect the practice of pursuing wealth or influence when making such matches?

Y.S. No, there is nothing very wrong in it.

Str. But when we are specially concerned with the very people who make much of being "well connected," justice re-

c quires that we should be all the more outspoken if we find them acting unsuitably.

Y.S. That is reasonable.

Str. They do not act on any sound or self-consistent principle. See how they pursue the immediate satisfaction of their desire by hailing with delight those who are like themselves and by disliking those who are different. Thus they assign far too great an importance to their own dislikes.

Y.S. In what way?

Str. The moderate natures look for a partner like themselves, and, so far as they can, they choose their wives from women of this quiet type. When they have daughters to bestow in marriage, once again they look for this type of character in the prospective husband. The courageous class does just the same thing and looks for natures of the same type. Yet both types should be doing exactly the opposite. d

Y.S. How can they, and why should they?

Str. Because if a courageous nature is reproduced for many generations without any admixture of the moderate type, the natural course of development is that at first it becomes superlatively powerful but in the end it breaks out into sheer madness.

Y.S. That is to be expected.

Str. But the soul which is too full of modesty and untinged by valor and audacity, if reproduced after its kind for many generations, becomes too dull to respond to the challenges of life and in the end becomes quite incapable of acting at all. e

Y.S. Yes, this is also the result one would expect.

Str. I repeat what I was saying. There is no difficulty in forging these bonds if both classes start out with one and the same conviction about what is honorable and good. There is one absorbing preoccupation for the kingly weaver as he makes the web of state. He must never permit the self-controlled characters to be separated from the brave ones; to avoid this he must make the fabric close and firm by weaving common convictions in them, and by making public honors and triumphs subserve this end; and finally, each must be involved with the other in the solemn pledges of matrimony. When he has woven his web smooth and "close woven,"[50] as the phrase goes, out of men of these differing types, he must entrust the various offices of state to them to be shared in all cases between them. 311

[50] There seems to be a quotation intended. The word survives in a fragment of Aeschylus' *Fishermen* (fr. 47) but is otherwise only cited from authors later than Plato.

Y.S. How can he do this?

Str. When a single magistrate happens to be needed, a man possessing both characteristics must be chosen and set in authority. Where several magistrates are wanted, he must bring together some representatives of each type to share the duties. Magistrates of the self-controlled type are exceedingly cautious, just, and conservative of precedent; but they lack pungency and the drive which makes for efficiency.

Y.S. Yes, that certainly seems to be the case.

b *Str.* The courageous type for their part have far less of the gifts of justice and caution than the others, but they have in a marked degree the drive that gets things done. A state can never function well either in the personal affairs of its citizens or in its public activities unless both of these elements of character are present.

Y.S. Of course that is so.

Str. Now we have reached the end of weaving the web of political action. The strands run true and are the gentle and the brave. Here these strands are woven together into a unified c character. For this unity is won where the kingly art draws the life of both types into a true fellowship by mutual concord and by ties of friendship. It is the finest and best of all fabrics. It enfolds all who dwell in the city, slave or free, in its firm contexture. Its kingly weaver maintains his control and oversight over it, and it lacks nothing that makes for happiness so far as happiness is obtainable in a state.

Socrates. You have drawn to perfection, Sir, a picture of the true king and statesman.